An introduction to building Python GUIs with PyQt6

Paul Hill

Cover by author.

For Laurence and Amelie

And all those who have encouraged me including:

Jo, Barbie, Alan, Jane, Brittany & Chris,
and Theo who would really rather just play tug-o-war!

Other books by **Paul Hill** include:

A beginner's guide to adding a GUI to your Python Programs using Tkinter.

Contents

Who is this book for?

This book is intended to be a quick start for people who already know Python and want to learn to create a graphical user interface (GUI) using PyQt6. I have previously written a beginners guide to creating a GUI for Python using Tkinter, the standard Python interface to the Tcl/Tk GUI toolkit. I recognise that having learned Tkinter, some people will wish to advance to PyQt and some will wish to bypass Tkinter and move straight to PyQt.

What is Qt?

Qt (pronounced 'cute') is a GUI toolkit developed by the Qt Group a Finnish software company (formerly Trolltech and Quasar Technologies) that allows development of applications across multiple platforms (Win, Mac, Linux, Mobile etc). Qt is written in C++.

Qt includes both standard GUI elements (buttons, labels, menus etc) whilst also including advanced elements for 3D graphics, multimedia, networking, and other features.

Qt provides a range of tools for both designing and then building graphical user interfaces,

Qt is a powerful and very flexible toolkit used for creating cross-platform applications with a rich graphical user interface. It is a popular choice for developers looking to create modern and responsive applications.

Why Qt rather than Tkinter?

Both Tkinter and Qt are both good options and each has it's own advantages and disadvantages. I have used both. Tkinter is built-in to Python, has a smaller memory footprint and is easier to get started with. PyQt has the amazing Qt Designer, a more comprehensive set of Widgets and perhaps better cross-platform support.

What are PyQt6 and PySide6?

PySide6 and PyQt6 (pronounced 'pie cute 6') are both Python bindings* for the Qt framework, which means that they have access to the same set of widgets and tools provided by the Qt framework. This includes a wide range of pre-built widgets for creating GUIs, such as buttons, text boxes, sliders, checkboxes, tables, and more.

The API for both libraries is also very similar, which means that most of the code you write for one library will also work with the other. This means that you can use the same set of widgets and tools with either library, and that code examples and documentation for one library will also be applicable to the other.

However, there may be some differences in the implementation details between the two libraries, particularly in areas that are not part of the Qt API. For example, PyQt6 may have some additional features or capabilities that are not present in PySide6, or vice versa. Additionally, there may be some differences in how the two libraries handle certain edge cases or unusual situations.

Overall, the widgets and tools provided by the Qt framework are available to both PySide6 and PyQt6, and the two libraries are generally interchangeable in terms of their capabilities and features. Here is a piece of knowledge for trivia fans: "Side' is Finnish for binding. In 2009, Nokia, the then owners of the Qt toolkit, wanted a Python binding available under the LGPL license. Nokia failed to reach an agreement with Riverbank Computing (the developers of the PyQt Python binding) and so in August, Nokia released PySide which provided similar functionality, but under the LGPL. For the purposes of this book, we'll concentrate on PyQt6.

*What are Bindings?

In software development, a binding is a mechanism for connecting code written in one programming language to code written in another programming language. The goal of a binding is to allow code written in one language to interact with code written in another language as if they were written in the same language.

Bindings are typically used to connect applications or libraries written in different languages. For example, Python bindings for C++ libraries are commonly used to allow Python code to use the functionality provided by C++ libraries such as Qt.

What is the difference between GPL and LGPL

GPL (General Public License) and LGPL (Lesser General Public License) are both open-source software licenses that grant users certain rights and freedoms to use, modify, and distribute the software. The key difference between GPL and LGPL is in the way they handle software dependencies.

GPL is a copyleft license, which means that any software that is derived from GPL-licensed code must also be licensed under the GPL, and any modifications to the code must be released under the same license. This can be a concern for some software developers who want to use GPL-licensed code in their projects, as it may require them to release their own code under the GPL as well.

LGPL, on the other hand, is a more permissive license that allows software that links to LGPL-licensed code to be distributed under any license. This means that you can use LGPL-licensed code in your own projects without having to release your own code under the LGPL or any other open-source license. However, if you modify the LGPL-licensed code itself, those modifications must be released under the LGPL.

In summary, GPL is more restrictive and requires derivative works to be licensed under the same terms, while LGPL is more permissive and allows for more flexibility in how the software can be used and distributed. The choice between GPL and LGPL will depend on the specific needs and goals of your project.

What is PyQt?

PyQt is a Python binding for the QT GUI toolkit (see below). **PyQt** allows users to develop Python applications with GUI that can run on various platforms such as Windows, Mac, and Linux.

The QtGui module provides GUI elements like windows, buttons, menus and text fields.

PyQt also provides support for many other services including multimedia, network programming, database access, and web services which are not covered in this book.

PyQt is available under a dual license model: the GPL (General Public License) and a commercial license. This means that developers can use PyQt for free under the terms of the GPL, or they can purchase a commercial license for proprietary software development.

PyQt6 Modules

PyQt6.QtCore, **PyQt6.QtGui**, and **PyQt6.QtWidgets** are modules in the PyQt6 library that provide different types of functionality for building graphical user interfaces (GUIs) using the Qt framework.

PyQt6.QtCore: This module provides core non-GUI functionality such as signals and slots for communication between objects, event handling, timers, and other basic features.

PyQt6.QtGui: This module provides classes for building the graphical elements of a GUI, such as windows, menus, buttons, text boxes, and other controls.

PyQt6.QtWidgets: This module provides a set of high-level GUI elements, such as dialogs, layouts, and other widgets that can be used to build complex GUI applications.

In general, **PyQt6.QtCore** provides the foundation for building PyQt6 applications, **PyQt6.QtGui** provides the low-level graphical elements of the GUI, and **PyQt6.QtWidgets** provides high-level widgets that can be used to create more complex GUI applications. By using these modules together, developers can build robust and powerful GUI applications using the Qt framework.

Designing the User Interface

A great user interface (UI) is one that is user-friendly, visually appealing, and efficient. Here are some of the characteristics of a great UI to think about whilst you are working with PyQt:

Consistency: A great UI should be consistent in its design, layout, and behaviour throughout the application. This makes it easier for users to navigate and understand the interface.

Clarity: The interface should be clear and easy to understand, with intuitive navigation and clear labelling of buttons and other elements. This helps users to quickly understand how to use the application.

Responsiveness: A great UI should be responsive to user actions, providing quick feedback and updates to the user as they interact with the application.

Simplicity: The interface should be simple and uncluttered, with a clean and minimalist design that makes it easy for users to focus on the task at hand.

Customisable: The interface should allow users to customise the interface to their preferences, such as changing the font size or colour scheme.

Accessibility: The interface should provide accessibility options to users with different abilities and disabilities, such as by providing keyboard shortcuts.

Visual appeal: The interface should be visually appealing, with a design that is both aesthetically pleasing and engaging to users.

Overall, a great UI is one that is designed with the end user in mind, making it easy, intuitivo, and efficient for them to use the application.

Creating an account and downloading software

If you start at the Qt Company website

https://www.qt.io/

you will be able to create an account and download the software you need.

The Qt framework is available under both open source and commercial licenses. This dual-licensing model is based on the principal of quid pro quo – roughly meaning "something for something."

In return for the value you receive from using Qt to create your application, you are expected to give back by contributing to Qt or buying Q

The examples in this book

This book will explain how to create GUI elements using example code. This code has been tested using PyQt6 v6.5.0 with Python 3.10/3.11 running on a Windows 11 PC. If you need to use older versions of either Python or PyQt, some of the code will likely require modification.

In order to keep things as simple as possible in the examples, I haven't used Object Oriented Programming (OOP) in this book.

A few acronyms

GPL General Public Licence

GUI Graphical User Interface

IDE Integrated Development Environment

LGPL Lesser General Public License

PyRCC Python Resource Compiler for Qt

PyQt The Python Interface to Qt

PySide An alternative set of Python bindings for Qt

QRC Qt Resource Collection

Qt A recursive name meaning Qt Toolkit. Pronounced "Cute"

TCL Tool Command Language

Tk Tool Kit a GUI Library developed for **TCL**

Tkinter The Python interface for **Tk**

Ttk Themed Tkinter

UIC User Interface Compiler (converts the PyQt XML to Python)

XML eXtensible Markup Language

Why learn PyQt? – A Story

Once upon a time, there was a girl named Amelie who loved to create beautiful graphical user interfaces (GUIs). She started her journey by learning the basics of GUI development using the Python library called Tkinter. She learned how to create buttons, text fields, labels, and other widgets, and she built some simple applications to practice her skills.

Amelie was always passionate about technology and how it can help solve real-world problems. She was always fascinated by how software could be used to create beautiful and intuitive user interfaces that could make people's lives easier. That's why she was drawn to GUI development and decided to learn Python's Tkinter library to start her journey.

Amelie spent countless hours practicing and experimenting with Tkinter, and she was able to create some simple applications. As she continued to develop her skills, she realized that Tkinter had some limitations that made it difficult to create more complex and modern-looking applications.

That's when she started to explore other GUI libraries that could help her take her skills to the next level. After some research, she came across PyQt, a powerful and versatile GUI library that was built on top of Qt, a popular C++ GUI framework.

Amelie was intrigued by PyQt's capabilities and decided to give it a try. She started by learning the basics of PyQt and how it differs from Tkinter. She learned that PyQt had a steeper learning curve and a more complex syntax, but it also offered many advanced features that could help her create more complex and responsive applications.

To make the learning process easier, Amelie decided to use PyQt Designer, a visual tool that allowed her to create GUI layouts by dragging and dropping widgets onto a canvas. She found it to be an incredibly useful tool that saved her time and effort, and she was able to create some beautiful layouts that looked great on different platforms.

But learning PyQt Designer was just the beginning. Amelie also had to learn how to work with signals and slots, PyQt's mechanism for event handling. She had to learn how to create custom widgets, a powerful feature that allowed her to create more specialised and reusable components. She also had to learn how to design custom stylesheets to give her applications a unique look and feel.

The learning process was challenging and often frustrating, but Amelie was determined to master PyQt. She spent hours practicing, reading documentation, and watching tutorials. She also joined online communities and forums to ask for help and advice.

As she progressed, Amelie started to see the benefits of using PyQt. She was able to create some amazing applications that impressed her friends and colleagues.

Amelie was thrilled with her progress and grateful for the opportunity to learn a new library that expanded her horizons. She realised that there was always something new to learn and that the world of GUI development was constantly evolving. She was excited to continue learning and exploring other GUI libraries that could help her create even more amazing applications in the future.

Despite her success, Amelie remained humble and sensitive to the needs of others. She was always willing to lend a hand to her colleagues and friends and was grateful for the opportunity to learn from their experiences as well.

Overall, Amelie's sensitivity, thoughtfulness, and intelligence made her a skilled and compassionate developer who was always looking for ways to use technology to make a positive impact on people's lives.

Creating a Virtual Environment

Creating a virtual environment is a recommended best practice when working on multiple Python projects or collaborating with other developers, as it helps to ensure that each project has its own isolated environment with its own dependencies and packages. This helps avoid conflicts and compatibility issues between different projects.

A Python virtual environment is a self-contained directory that contains a specific version of Python, along with all the dependencies and packages required for a particular project.

To create a virtual environment, you can use the built-in venv module in Python 3. The basic steps are as follows:

Firstly open your terminal or command prompt and then Navigate to the directory where you want to create the virtual environment.

Python -m venv (directory)

Install any packages or dependencies required for your project using:

pip install (package)

When you're finished working on the project, deactivate the virtual environment by running the command deactivate.

By using virtual environments, you can easily switch between different Python environments and ensure that each project has its own isolated set of dependencies and packages.

Activating a virtual environment

Activate the virtual environment by running the command source myenv/bin/activate (or myenv\Scripts\activate on Windows). Where **myenv** is the location of the virtual environment that you created.

activate

When you activate a Python virtual environment, the name of the environment will be added to your command prompt, indicating that the environment is active.

The exact format of the command prompt will depend on your operating system and shell. Example:

(myenv) C:\Users\user\project>

Deactivating a virtual environment

Deactivate

In addition to the command prompt, you can also check if a virtual environment is active by using the which or where command to see the location of the python executable. When a virtual environment is active, this location will point to the python executable within the virtual environment's directory.

Installing PyQt

If you haven't done so already, you will need to install PyQt. Unlike Tkinter, PyQt is not part of the standard Python distribution.

I'm working on a Windows 11 PC with Windows and Python already installed so the command to install PyQt6 is:

pip install pyqt6

You can check that it is installed with the following command from the command prompt:

pip show pyqt6

Which will produce something like:

```
Name: PyQt6
Version: 6.5.0
Summary: Python bindings for the Qt cross platform application toolkit
Home-page: https://www.riverbankcomputing.com/software/pyqt/
Author: Riverbank Computing Limited
Author-email: info@riverbankcomputing.com
License: GPL v3
Location:
c:\users\paul_\appdata\local\packages\pythonsoftwarefoundation.python.3.
10_qbz5n2kfra8p0\localcache\local-packages\python310\site-packages
Requires: PyQt6-Qt6, PyQt6-sip
Required-by: PyQt6-WebEngine
```

Or from the Python prompt:

```
import PyQt6
from PyQt6 import QtCore
print(PyQt6.QtCore.PYQT_VERSION_STR)
```

Output:

6.5.0

Hello World!

We will start in the traditional way with example code for a very Simple "Hello World!" example program:

```
from PyQt6.QtWidgets import QApplication, QLabel
app = QApplication([])
my_label = QLabel("Hello World!")
my_label.show()
app.exec()
```

Output:

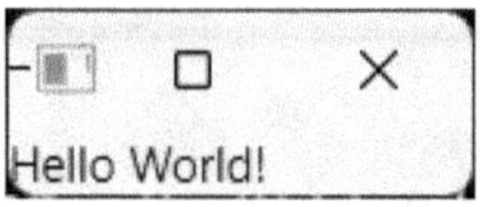

from PyQt6.QtWidgets import QApplication, QLabel this line imports two classes from PyQt6

QApplication is a class in the PyQt library that represents the main application window of a PyQt-based graphical user interface (GUI) application. **QApplication** can take a number of optional arguments that control the application and it's style (more on these later). The arguments would be in a list of strings but as we don't have any arguments in this example we provide an empty list as shown by the square brackets **[]**.

QLabel is a widget class that is used to display text or an image on the screen. It can be used to create a simple label as in this case, or a more complex one that can display HTML-formatted text, rich text, or even a movie. More detail on **QLabel** later in the book.

mylabel.show() - the **show()** method is used to display a widget on the screen. It is a method of the **QWidget** class, which is the base class for all user interface objects in PyQt. When you call **show()** on a widget, PyQt creates a new window and displays the widget in that window. The widget is then made visible on the screen.

app.exec() is a method of the QApplication class that starts the application's event loop and waits for events to be processed. The **exec()** method blocks the main thread of the application and does not return until the QApplication object is destroyed or the **exit()** method is called.

Hello World! (2)

That first example was a very basic bare-bones example. I have created a 2nd Hello World example which is better commented and begins to bring in a few more elements that would appear in a typical Python **PyQt** application, notably:

import sys - the **sys** module provides access to some variables and functions that interact with the Python interpreter. In this case we are used going to use it to exit the Python interpreter when we are finished with our window. The things you can do with **sys** include:

> **Access command-line arguments**: The **sys.argv** variable is a list that contains the command-line arguments passed to your Python script.
>
> **Exit the program**: The **sys.exit()** function allows you to exit the Python interpreter.
>
> **Access system-specific parameters**: The **sys.platform** variable contains a string that identifies the operating system on which the Python interpreter is running.

We have a specific layout using the **PyQt6 QVBoxLayout** layout manager (Vertical Box Layout) to control how our widgets are arranged. This is explained more in the following chapter "Windows Layout".

The Window has a title and a specific size using the commands:

window.setWindowTitle("Hello World!")
window.resize(250, 150)

window.resize() is a method of the QWidget class that sets the size of a window or widget. The **window.resize** method is used to resize a **QMainWindow** or **QDialog** widget. This method takes two arguments, width and height, which specify the new width and height of the widget in pixels.

Example:

```
import sys
from PyQt6.QtWidgets import QApplication, QLabel, QVBoxLayout,
QWidget

# Create a new application instance
app = QApplication(sys.argv)

# Create a new window
window = QWidget()

# Create a label with "Hello World!" text
label = QLabel("Hello World!")

# Create a vertical layout and add the label to it
```

```
layout = QVBoxLayout() # Vertical Column
layout.addWidget(label)

# Set the layout of the window to the vertical layout
window.setLayout(layout)

# Set the size and title of the window
window.setWindowTitle("Hello World!")
window.resize(250, 150)

# Show the window
window.show()
```

Output:

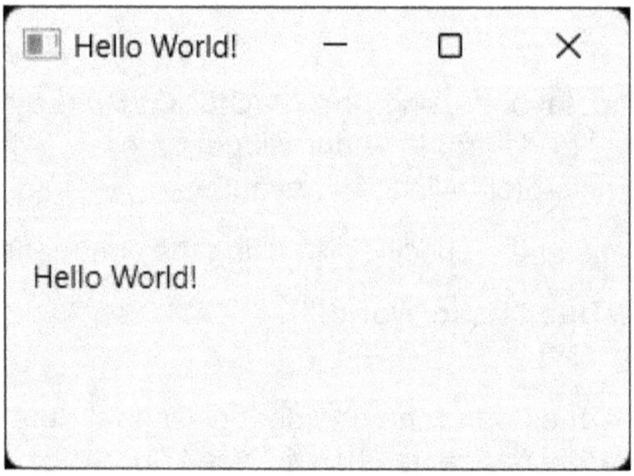

QMainWindow

In PyQt6, **QMainWindow** is a class that provides a main application window with a menu bar, toolbars, and a central widget area. It is a subclass of **QWidget**, so it inherits all of the functionality provided by **QWidge**t, such as setting the window title and geometry.

QMainWindow is designed to be used as the main window of an application. It includes a **QMenuBar** object for creating menus, as well as **QToolBar** objects for creating toolbars. The central widget area is used for displaying the main content of the application, such as a text editor or a canvas for drawing.

Example:
In this example, we create an instance of **QMainWindow** called main_window. We set the window's title and size using the **setWindowTitle()** and **setGeometry()** methods, respectively. We also create a **QLabel** widget to use as the central widget for the window, and set it using the **setCentralWidget()** method. **setCentralWidget** is a method of **QMainWindow** class that sets the central widget of the main window. The central widget is the primary widget that occupies the central area of the main window. An alternative to **setCentralWidget** is to use a layout manager to add widgets to the central area of the main window. Layout managers (*see section PyQt6 Layout Managers)* are used to arrange widgets in a container widget such as a **QMainWindow**. You can create a layout, add widgets to it, and then set the layout as the central layout of the main window using the **setCentralWidge**t method.

The **setGeometry() method** is a common method in PyQt6 used to set the position and size of a widget or window. It allows you to specify the dimensions and location of a widget within its parent or on the desktop screen.

The syntax for **setGeometry()** is as follows:

widget.setGeometry(x, y, width, height)

Finally, we show the window, start the event loop, and run the application. When the application is run, it will display a window with the label *"This is a QLabel in the Main Window. Use the File Menu to Exit"* in the center.

```
import sys
from PyQt6.QtWidgets import QApplication, QMainWindow, QLabel,
QMenu
from PyQt6.QtGui import QAction

# Create a new QApplication instance
app = QApplication(sys.argv)

# Create an instance of QMainWindow
main_window = QMainWindow()
main_window.setWindowTitle("My Main Window")
main_window.setGeometry(100, 100, 350, 150)
```

```
# Create a central widget for the main window
central_widget = QLabel("This is a QLabel in the Main Window. Use the File Menu to Exit")
main_window.setCentralWidget(central_widget)

# Create a File menu
file_menu = main_window.menuBar().addMenu("File")

# Create an Exit action and add it to the File menu
exit_action = QAction("Exit", main_window)
exit_action.setShortcut("Ctrl+Q")
exit_action.triggered.connect(main_window.close)
file_menu.addAction(exit_action)

# Show the window
main_window.show()

# Run the event loop
sys.exit(app.exec())
```

Output:

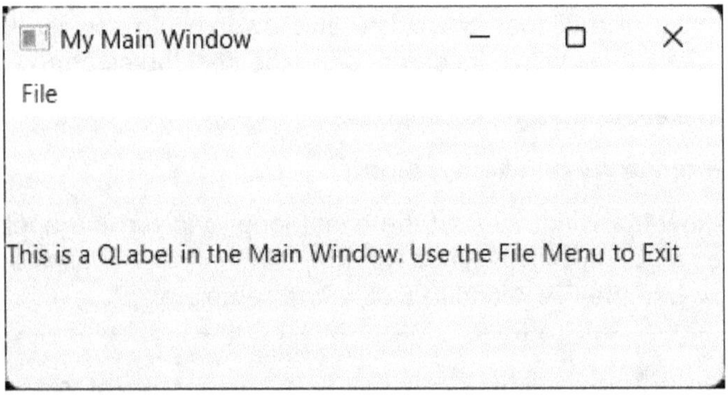

QtWidgets

The **QtWidgets** module provides a set of classes and functions for creating graphical user interfaces. It includes a wide range of widgets, such as windows, dialogs, buttons, labels, text boxes, and many others. The **QtWidgets** module is part of the Qt toolkit, which is a cross-platform application framework for developing graphical user interfaces.

Some of the key classes provided by the QtWidgets module include:

QApplication: The application object that manages the application's event loop and main window. *See next section.*

QWidget: The base class for all user interface elements, providing a set of methods and properties for managing graphical elements.

QMainWindow: A main application window that can contain menus, toolbars, and a central widget area.

QDialog: A pop-up window that can be used to display messages or get user input. Typically used for those OK / Cancel Popups.

QPushButton: A clickable button that can be used to trigger actions or events.

QLabel: A static text label that displays text or images.

QLineEdit: A text box that allows the user to enter and edit text.

These are just a few examples of the many classes and functions provided by the QtWidgets module. These and many more are described later in the book.

QWidget

In **PyQt6**, both **QWidget** and **QMainWindow** (see above) are classes that can be used to create windows for your application. However, there are some differences between them.

QWidget is the base class for all user interface elements in **PyQt6**, including windows. It provides a set of methods and properties for managing graphical elements, but it does not include any built-in support for menus or toolbars. This means that you would need to create those components manually if you wanted to add them to a **QWidget**-based window.

QMainWindow, on the other hand, is a subclass of **QWidget** that provides additional functionality for creating main application windows. It includes support for menus, toolbars, and a central widget area. The central widget can be any subclass of **QWidget**, so you can add other widgets, such as buttons or text boxes, to the window as needed.

If you need a simple window without menus or toolbars, you can use **QWidget**. If you need a more complex window with menus and toolbars, you should use **QMainWindow**.

Syntax:

Import the required modules:

from PyQt6.QtWidgets import QApplication, QWidget

Create a QWidget instance

widget = QWidget()

Set the options

widget.setWindowTitle("Example")

Here are some commonly used methods of the **QWidget** class:

setGeometry(x: int, y: int, width: int, height: int) -> None	Sets the geometry (position and size) of the widget.
size() -> QSize	Returns the current size of the widget.
width() -> int	Returns the current width of the widget.
height() -> int	Returns the current height of the widget.
setVisible(visible: bool) -> None	Sets the visibility of the widget.
isEnabled() -> bool	Returns True if the widget is enabled; otherwise, returns False.
setEnabled(enabled: bool) -> None	Enables or disables the widget.
setStyleSheet(styleSheet: str) -> None	Sets the style sheet for the widget, allowing for customized styling and appearance.
setBackgroundRole(role: QPalette.ColorRole) -> None	Sets the background color role for the widget.
setAutoFillBackground(enabled: bool) -> None	Enables or disables automatic filling of the widget's background color.
setWindowTitle(title: str) -> None	Sets the title or caption for the widget's window.
setLayout(layout: QLayout) -> None	Sets the layout manager for the widget.
layout() -> QLayout	Returns the current layout manager of the widget.
show() -> None	Displays the widget on the screen.
hide() -> None	Hides the widget from the screen.
close() -> None	Closes the widget.

Example:

```
from PyQt6.QtWidgets import QApplication, QWidget, QPushButton
from PyQt6.QtCore import Qt
```

```
app = QApplication([])

# Create a QWidget instance
widget = QWidget()
widget.setWindowTitle("QWidget Example")
widget.setGeometry(100, 100, 300, 200)

# Create a QPushButton
button = QPushButton("Click me", widget)
button.setGeometry(100, 50, 100, 30)

# Set the background color and style sheet
widget.setAutoFillBackground(True)
palette = widget.palette()
palette.setColor(widget.backgroundRole(), Qt.GlobalColor.lightGray)
widget.setPalette(palette)
widget.setStyleSheet("QPushButton { background-color: yellow; }")

# Show the widget
widget.show()

app.exec()
```

Output:

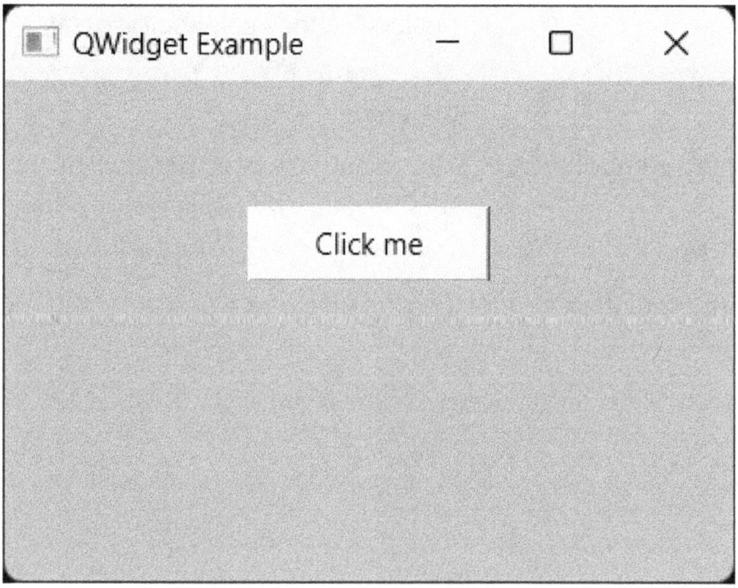

QApplication

QApplication is a class that represents the main application window of a PyQt-based graphical user interface (GUI) application.

QApplication creates and manages the application's event loop. The event loop is the main loop that processes user input, redraws the GUI, and handles other events.

The **QApplication** class provides methods to perform the following tasks:

- the **exec()** method to start the event loop and run the application.
- **QApplication** provides methods to set the application's settings including font, palette, style, and other settings.
- **QApplication** provides methods to manage application Windows including create, show, hide, and close windows.
- **QApplication** provides methods to handle global events such as keyboard shortcuts and system events.

QApplication Arguments

The **QApplication** constructor takes an optional list of command-line arguments as its argument. These arguments are passed to the underlying C++ application object, which can use them to modify the behavior of the application.

The common arguments that can be passed to **QApplication** include:

sys.argv	The command-line arguments passed to the Python script.
style <style>	The style to use for the widgets (e.g., Fusion, Windows, Macintosh, etc.).
stylesheet <file>	The path to a CSS file to use for styling the widgets.
geometry <geometry>	The initial size and position of the main window (e.g., 800x600+100+100).
font <font>	The default font to use for the widgets.
palette <palette>	The default palette to use for the widgets.

Alternatives to QApplication

In PyQt6, you can choose between three different application classes: **QApplication**, **QGuiApplication**, and **QCoreApplication.** The choice of which one to use depends on the type of application you're developing and the features you need.

QApplication: This class is suitable for traditional desktop applications with a graphical user interface (GUI). It provides event handling, window management, and other GUI-related functionalities. You should use QApplication when you want to create a desktop application with windows, dialogs, menus, toolbars, and other GUI components.

QGuiApplication: This class is similar to QApplication but is more lightweight. It is designed for applications that do not require a traditional desktop windowing system, such as console applications or applications with a custom rendering surface. QGuiApplication provides event handling, input management, and application-wide resources, but without the additional features related to windows and widgets.

QCoreApplication: This class is suitable for non-GUI applications or applications that do not require a user interface. It provides event handling and basic application functionalities but does not handle windows, GUI components, or input events. QCoreApplication is useful for developing command-line tools, services, or backend processes.

Here's a general guideline to help you choose the appropriate application class:

Use **QApplication** if you are developing a desktop application with a graphical user interface and need window management, event handling, and GUI-related functionalities.

Use **QGuiApplication** if you don't require the full set of features provided by QApplication and are developing a lightweight application without a traditional desktop windowing system.

Use **QCoreApplicatio**n if you are developing a non-GUI application, such as a command-line tool or a backend process, and don't need window management or GUI components.

In many cases, **QApplication** is the most commonly used choice for traditional desktop applications. However, if you are developing a different type of application or have specific requirements, you can choose the appropriate application class accordingly. Remember to import the correct application class from PyQt6.QtWidgets (QApplication and QGuiApplication) or PyQt6.QtCore (QCoreApplication) depending on your choice.

A more interesting example

My daughter has been learning Python at Primary School(!) and one of the first things that they have worked on is writing simple to control a virtual "turtle" (see *The BBC Turtle* overleaf). The Python Turtle module is a built-in graphics module in Python that allows you to create graphics and shapes by controlling a virtual turtle that moves around the screen. It's a fun and interactive way for beginners to learn programming concepts. As a way of explaining what I was writing about in this book, I worked with her to make a simple PyQt control panel to operate the turtle.

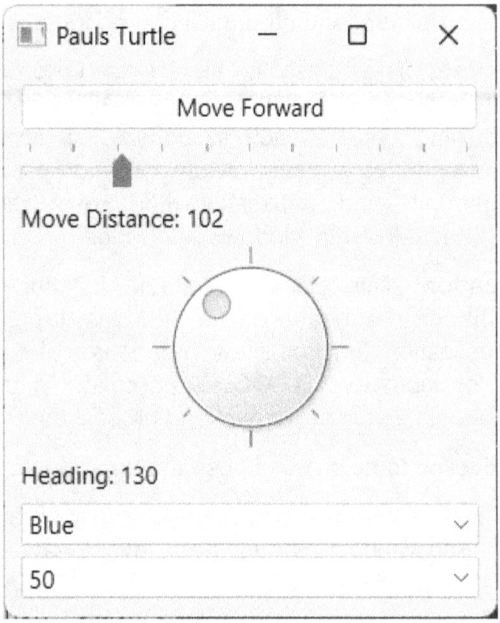

It may not be obvious, but this panel consists of a vertical stack of seven widgets. Theses widgets and many more are explained in more detail later in the book:

- A **QPushButton** that moves the turtle forward when pushed.
- A **QSlider** that sets how far the turtle will move.
- A **QLabel** that shows the value selected by the slider
- A **QDial** that controls the heading (direction in degrees) of the turtle.
- A **QLabel** that shows the value of the dial (turtle heading).
- A **QComboBox** that allows the turtle pen colour to be selected
- A **QComboBox** that allows the turtle pen width to be selected

There are clearly a lot of other features I could have added to my control panel but if you look at the sample code below, you will see that it is super easy to add more.

Example Code:

```
from PyQt6.QtWidgets import *
from PyQt6.QtCore import Qt
import turtle
```

```
app = QApplication([])
window = QMainWindow()
window.setWindowTitle('Pauls Turtle')
button = QPushButton('Move Forward')
speed_label = QLabel('Distance')
angle_label = QLabel('Heading')

tina = turtle.Turtle()
tina.shape('turtle')
tina.pendown()
tina.setheading(0)
turtle_move = 10 # how far does the turtle move
turtle_heading = 90 # direction turtle will move (degrees from x axis)

dial = QDial(window) # make a dial to set the turtle heading
dial.setOrientation(Qt.Orientation.Vertical)
dial.setMinimum(0) # Set the minimum and maximum values for the dial
dial.setMaximum(359) # 0 to 359 degrees
dial.setGeometry(50, 50, 100, 100) # Set the size and position of the dial
dial.setWrapping(True) # allows the dial to rotate past 360 degrees
dial.setInvertedAppearance(True) # make the dial work anticlockwise
dial.setNotchesVisible(True)
dial.setNotchSize(20)
dial.setSingleStep(45)
dial.setValue(90)

slider = QSlider() # slider to select turtle move distance
slider.setOrientation(Qt.Orientation.Horizontal)
slider.setMinimum(0) # set the range of values
slider.setMaximum(500)
slider.setValue(0) # set the start position of the slider
slider.setTickPosition(QSlider.TickPosition.TicksAbove)
slider.setTickInterval(50)
slider.setSingleStep(10)
slider.setTracking(True)

pen_colour = QComboBox() # combobox to select pen colour
pen_colour.addItem("Black")
pen_colour.addItem("Blue")
pen_colour.addItem("Green")
pen_colour.addItem("Red")
pen_colour.addItem("Yellow")
```

```
pen_colour.addItem("Pink")
pen_colour.setCurrentIndex(1)

pen_width = QComboBox() # combobox to select pen width in pixels
pen_width.addItem("1")
pen_width.addItem("5")
pen_width.addItem("10")
pen_width.addItem("15")
pen_width.addItem("25")
pen_width.addItem("50")
pen_width.setCurrentIndex(1)

def slider_moved(value):
        global turtle_move
        turtle_move = slider.value()
        speed_label.setText("Move Distance: {}".format(value))

def dial_turned(value):
        global turtle_heading
        turtle_heading = dial.value()
        turtle_heading = (turtle_heading - 90) %360 # align turtle with dial
        tina.setheading(turtle_heading)
        angle_label.setText("Heading: {}".format(turtle_heading))

def button_pushed():
        global turtle_move
        tina.forward(turtle_move)

def pen_change():
        tina.pencolor(pen_colour.currentText())

def width_changed():
        tina.pensize(pen_width.currentText())

# detect controls moved
slider.valueChanged.connect(slider_moved) # detect slider moved
dial.valueChanged.connect(dial_turned) # detect dial turned
button.clicked.connect(button_pushed) # detect button being pushed
pen_colour.currentIndexChanged.connect(pen_change) # detect colour
change
pen_width.currentIndexChanged.connect(width_changed) # detect pen
width change
```

```
layout = QVBoxLayout()
layout.addWidget(button)
layout.addWidget(slider)
layout.addWidget(speed_label)
layout.addWidget(dial)
layout.addWidget(angle_label)
layout.addWidget(pen_colour)
layout.addWidget(pen_width)

central_widget = QWidget()
central_widget.setLayout(layout)
window.setCentralWidget(central_widget)

slider_moved(0)
dial_turned(0)

window.show()
app.exec()
```

The BBC Turtle

The turtle in the code above is a virtual turtle appearing on a computer monitor. It is based on the concept of a "Turtle" robot – so called because of the protective dome covering the mechanism. For those who don't remember.... The BBC Microcomputer Turtle (possibly a Ralph Jessops Turtle) was a small domed robot programmed using the LOGO programming language.

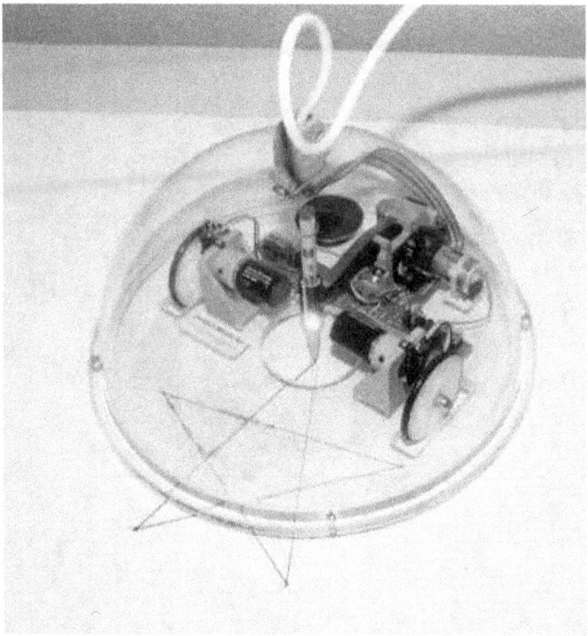

Inside the dome, there were a couple of stepper motors for the driving wheels and a motor for applying or retracting the Pen.

Image courtesy of "The Centre for Computing History" (CCH).

PyQt6 Layout Managers

PyQt6 has a number of different methods of organising widgets within a window. For a more complex project you will want to look at the drag and drop Qt designer tool (see further below) but there are some simple options including **QVBoxLayout**, **QHBoxLayout**, **QGridLayout and QFormLayout** which are ideal for many simply GUI designs. If you want something more complex, you may wish to look at using the **Qt Designer** software package (*see later section on designing a GUI with QT Designer*).

Note that with the horizontal and vertical box layouts, the order in which widgets are added to the layout determines their placement within the layout. Widgets are arranged in the order they are added, from top to bottom. If you want to control the spacing between widgets, you can use the **addSpacing()** method to add a fixed amount of space between them, or the **addStretch()** method to add a stretchable space that expands or contracts to fill available space.

QVBoxLayout Vertical Box Layout

```
my_layout = QVBoxLayout() # create vertical layout
my_layout.addWidget(widget1) # add widgets to the layout
my_layout.addWidget(widget2)
my_layout.addWidget(widget3)
window.setLayout(my_layout)
```

QHBoxLayout Horizontal Box Layout

```
my_layout = QHBoxLayout() # create horizontal layout
my_layout.addWidget(widget1) # add widgets to the layout
my_layout.addWidget(widget2)
my_layout.addWidget(widget3)
window.setLayout(my_layout)
```

Grid Layout is very similar except that when you add the widgets to the layout, you also specify the row an column in which you want to place them.

QGridLayout

To create a layout like this, widgets are placed by row and column starting from 0. So in this example, Widgets1 and 2 are in Row 0 Columns 0 and 1.

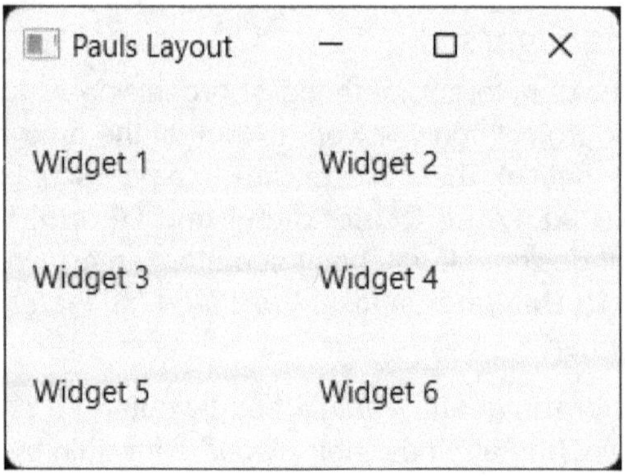


```
my_layout = QGridLayout() # create Grid layout
my_layout.addWidget(widget1, 0, 0)
my_layout.addWidget(widget2, 0, 1)
my_layout.addWidget(widget3, 1, 0)
my_layout.addWidget(widget4, 1, 1)
my_layout.addWidget(widget5, 2, 0)
my_layout.addWidget(widget6, 2, 1)
window.setLayout(my_layout)
```

To make things a bit more interesting and more flexible, you can nest these layouts within each other.

I will provide a simple example showing a Horizontal layout nested within a vertical layout.

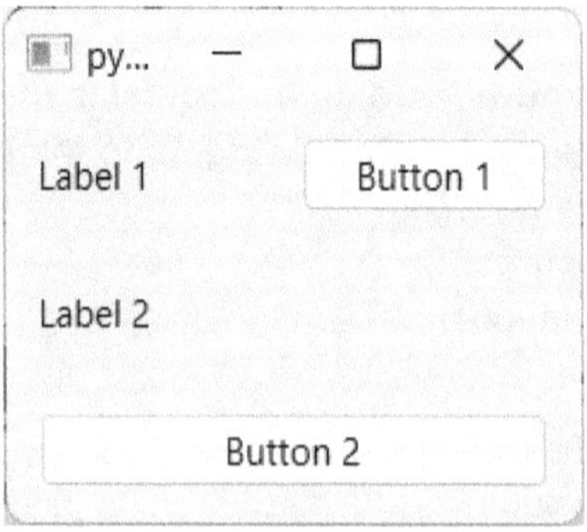

Example code:

```
import sys
from PyQt6.QtWidgets import QApplication, QWidget, QVBoxLayout,
QHBoxLayout, QLabel, QPushButton

app = QApplication(sys.argv)
window = QWidget()

# Create vertical layout for the window
vertical_layout = QVBoxLayout()

# Create horizontal layout for the top of the window
horizontal_layout = QHBoxLayout()

# Create label and button widgets
label1 = QLabel("Label 1")
button1 = QPushButton("Button 1")
label2 = QLabel("Label 2")
button2 = QPushButton("Button 2")

# Add widgets to horizontal layout
horizontal_layout.addWidget(label1)
horizontal_layout.addWidget(button1)

# Add horizontal layout to vertical layout
vertical_layout.addLayout(horizontal_layout)

# Add widgets to vertical layout
vertical_layout.addWidget(label2)
vertical_layout.addWidget(button2)

# Set the main layout of the window
window.setLayout(vertical_layout)

# Show the window
window.show()
sys.exit(app.exec())
```

QFormLayout

QFormLayout is a layout manager provided by PyQt6 that arranges widgets in a two-column form-like structure.

QFormLayout is particularly useful when you need to design forms or input dialogs with labelled fields. It automatically positions labels on the left side and associated widgets on the right side. This layout is commonly used for inputting or displaying data that requires labels for clarity.

Syntax:

The following modules are required

from PyQt6.QtWidgets import QApplication, QFormLayout, QLabel, QLineEdit, QWidget

Setup the layout

my_layout = QFormLayout()

Add the widgets to the QFormLayout using the **addRow()** method:

my_layout.addRow(label1, line_edit1)

my_layout.addRow(label2, line_edit2)

Create a parent QWidget and set the QFormLayout as its layout:

widget = QWidget()

widget.setLayout(form_layout)

Methods:

addRow(label: QWidget, field: QWidget)	Adds a labelled field to the layout. The label parameter is a widget used as the label or description for the field, and the field parameter is the widget associated with the label.
addRow(labelText: str, field: QWidget)	Adds a labelled field to the layout using a text string as the label. The labelText parameter is the text to be displayed as the label.
insertRow(row: int, label: QWidget, field: QWidget)	Inserts a labelled field at a specific row index in the layout.

insertRow(row: int, labelText: str, field: QWidget)	Inserts a labelled field at a specific row index using a text string as the label.
removeRow(row: int)	Removes the labelled field at the specified row index from the layout.
setAlignment(field: QWidget, alignment: Qt.Alignment)	Sets the alignment of a specific field widget within the layout. The alignment parameter specifies the desired alignment using Qt.Alignment values.
setLabelAlignment(alignment: Qt.Alignment)	Sets the alignment of all the labels within the layout. The alignment parameter specifies the desired alignment using Qt.Alignment values.
setSpacing(spacing: int)	Sets the spacing between rows in the layout. The spacing parameter specifies the desired spacing in pixels.
rowCount() -> int	Returns the total number of rows in the layout.
labelForField(field: QWidget) -> QLabel	Returns the QLabel associated with the specified field widget, if one exists.
fieldForRow(row: int) -> QWidget	Returns the QWidget associated with the labelled field at the specified row index.

First simple example:

```
from PyQt6.QtWidgets import QApplication, QFormLayout, QLabel,
QLineEdit, QWidget

app = QApplication([])

# create the layout
form_layout = QFormLayout()
```

```
# create the labels and line edit for each row
label1 = QLabel("Name")
line_edit1 = QLineEdit()

label2 = QLabel("Address")
line_edit2 = QLineEdit()

label3 = QLabel("Postcode")
line_edit3 = QLineEdit()

label4 = QLabel("Email Address")
line_edit4 = QLineEdit()

# add the rows to the layout
form_layout.addRow(label1, line_edit1)
form_layout.addRow(label2, line_edit2)
form_layout.addRow(label3, line_edit3)
form_layout.addRow(label4, line_edit4)

widget = QWidget()
widget.setLayout(form_layout)

# Display the Widget
widget.show()
app.exec()
```

Output:

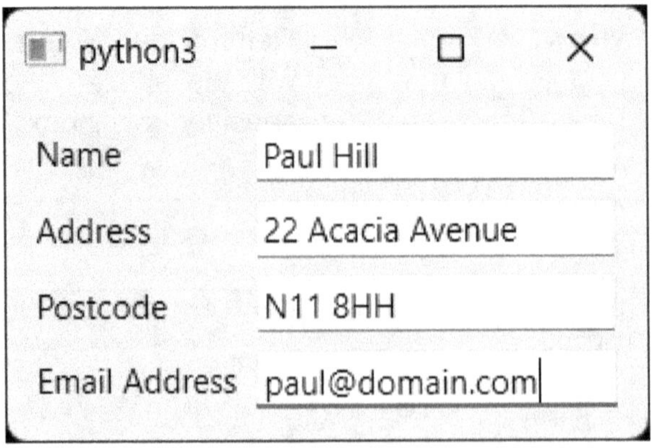

This second example takes it a little bit further adding a submit button to collect the data which is then printed to the console/terminal. You will see that the password is obscured on screen but is printed out in clear text.

```
from PyQt6.QtWidgets import QApplication, QFormLayout, QLabel,
QLineEdit, QPushButton, QVBoxLayout, QWidget

def submit_form():
    name = line_edit_name.text()
    email = line_edit_email.text()
    password = line_edit_password.text()

    print(f"Name: {name}")
    print(f"Email: {email}")
    print(f"Password: {password}")

app = QApplication([])

widget = QWidget()
layout = QVBoxLayout()
form_layout = QFormLayout()

label_name = QLabel("Name:")
line_edit_name = QLineEdit()

label_email = QLabel("Email:")
line_edit_email = QLineEdit()

label_password = QLabel("Password:")
line_edit_password = QLineEdit()
line_edit_password.setEchoMode(QLineEdit.EchoMode.Password)  # Hide
password input

button_submit = QPushButton("Submit")
button_submit.clicked.connect(submit_form)

form_layout.addRow(label_name, line_edit_name)
form_layout.addRow(label_email, line_edit_email)
form_layout.addRow(label_password, line_edit_password)

layout.addLayout(form_layout)
layout.addWidget(button_submit)

widget.setLayout(layout)
```

```
widget.show()

app.exec()
```

Output:

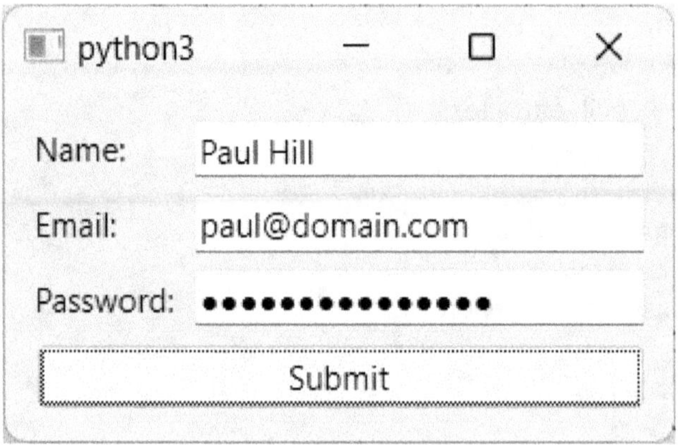

And to the console:

Name: Paul Hill

Email: paul@domain.com

Password: Secret Password

Text Alignment

In **PyQt6,** you can use the **setAlignment()** method to specify the text alignment for various widgets, such as **QLabel, QGroupBox, QPushButton**, etc. The **setAlignment()** method takes a **Qt.AlignmentFlag** as its argument, which can be one of the following values:

Qt.AlignLeft	Align the text to the left.
Qt.AlignRight	Align the text to the right.
Qt.AlignHCenter	Center the text horizontally.
Qt.AlignJustify	Justify the text.
Qt.AlignTop	Align the text to the top.
Qt.AlignBottom	Align the text to the bottom.
Qt.AlignVCenter	Center the text vertically.
Qt.AlignCenter	Center the text both horizontally and vertically.

To import **Qt** use **from PyQt6.QtCore import Qt**

Example:

```
from PyQt6.QtCore import Qt
from PyQt6.QtWidgets import QApplication, QLabel, QWidget,
QVBoxLayout

app = QApplication([])
window = QWidget()
layout = QVBoxLayout()

label = QLabel("Hello, PyQt6!")
label.setAlignment(Qt.AlignmentFlag.AlignCenter)  # center the text

layout.addWidget(label)
window.setLayout(layout)

window.show()
app.exec()
```

Output:

Signals and Slots

A user interface provides a way for the user to interact with the software. A great user interface is one that is user-friendly, visually appealing, and efficient.

It goes without saying that when the user pushes a button or turns a dial, they expect the software to respond to their input. In **PyQt**, signals and slots are a mechanism for communication between objects.

Signals are emitted by objects to indicate that a particular event has occurred. For example, a button might emit a signal when it is clicked, or a text box might emit a signal when the user enters some text.

Slots are functions that are called in response to a signal. When a signal is emitted, any connected slots are executed. For example, a slot might update the text in a label when the user enters text in a text box.

PyQt provides a convenient way to connect signals to slots using a simple syntax. For example, the following code connects a button's clicked signal to a slot that updates the text in a label:

Example:

```
from PyQt6.QtWidgets import *

app = QApplication([])
window = QMainWindow()
window.setWindowTitle('Slots and Signals')
button = QPushButton('Click me!')
label = QLabel('Button not clicked yet')

def update_label():
    label.setText('Button clicked!')

button.clicked.connect(update_label)

layout = QHBoxLayout() # Horizontal Row

layout.addWidget(button)
layout.addWidget(label)

central_widget = QWidget()
central_widget.setLayout(layout)
window.setCentralWidget(central_widget)

window.show()
app.exec()
```

In this example, the clicked signal of the button is connected to the **update_label** slot. When the button is clicked, the **update_label** function is called, which updates the text of the label widget to indicate that the button was clicked.

Signals and slots provide a powerful and flexible way to build responsive and interactive GUIs in **PyQt**. They allow the user interface to be decoupled from the underlying application logic, making it easier to maintain and modify complex applications.

Output:

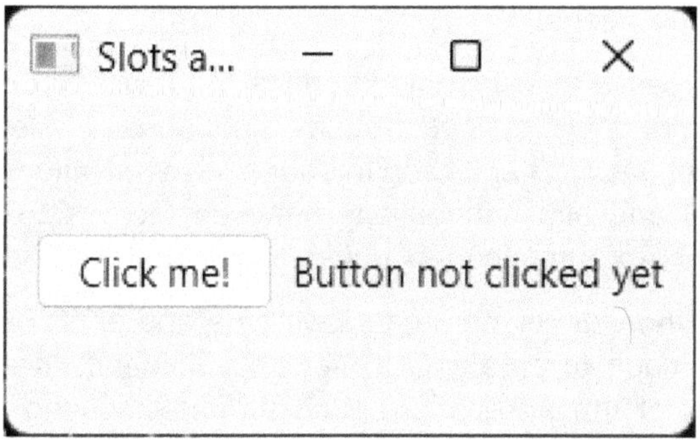

And after the button is clicked:

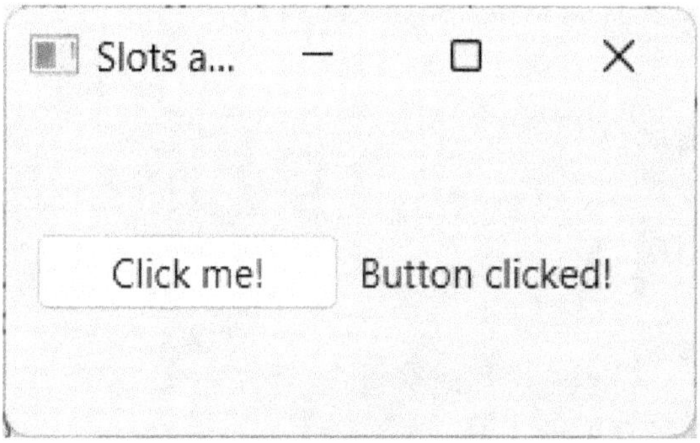

Designing a GUI using Qt Designer

PyQt provides tools for designing GUIs including **Qt Designer**. If you don't have it installed already: **pip install pyqt6-tools**

Qt Designer

Qt Designer is a graphical user interface (GUI) design tool that allows the creation and design of interfaces for applications using the Qt framework. **Qt Designer** is part of the Qt development toolkit, which is a cross-platform software development framework that provides developers with a set of tools for building desktop, mobile, and embedded applications.

Qt Designer provides a user-friendly interface to visually create and design GUI elements such as windows, dialogs, buttons, and labels. It allows arrangement of these elements using a drag-and-drop interface, customisations of their properties, and set up signal and slot connections between them. **Qt Designer** generates code in a variety of programming languages, including C++, Python, and Java.

By using **Qt Designer**, developers can save time and effort by avoiding the need to manually write code to create GUI elements. Instead, they can focus on the functional aspects of the application, such as implementing business logic and integrating with backend systems.

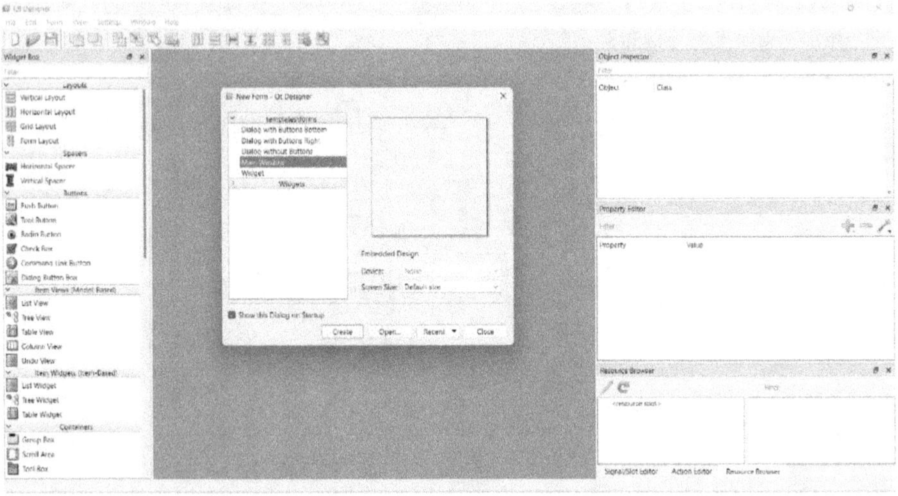

The files created by **QT Designer** are *.ui (user interface files). A Qt .ui file is an **XML** (eXtensible Markup Language) file that describes a user interface created with the **Qt Designer** tool. The .ui file contains a tree-like structure of widgets, including windows, buttons, labels, and other GUI elements.

The basic steps to create a **PyQt6 GUI** using the **Qt Designer** tool:

Open Qt Designer: Launch **Qt Designer** from your applications menu or by typing "designer" in your terminal. If not installed, you can download it from the official **PyQt6** website or install it using a package manager. E.g. **pip install pyqt6-tools**

Create a new form: In **Qt Designer**, go to "File" > "New" to create a new form. Choose the type of form you want to create, such as "Main Window" or "Dialog".

Add widgets: Drag and drop widgets from the left-hand side panel onto your form, such as buttons, labels, and text fields.

Customise widgets: Select a widget on your form and use the properties editor on the right-hand side panel to customise its appearance and behavior.

Save your form: When you're done designing your form, go to "File" > "Save" to save it as a .ui file.

The Qt Designer .UI Files

A Qt .ui file is a visual representation of a GUI that is created with the **Qt Designer** tool, and there are a couple of different ways that it can be used. it serves as an intermediate format that can be converted into executable code.

The .ui file can be used by a Python program (or any other language that supports Qt) by importing it and using it to create and customise the UI. The Qt framework provides tools to convert the .ui file into code that can be compiled and executed by the application. Alternatively, it is possible to load .ui files directly in your Python code using the **loadUi()** function provided by **PyQt**. Converting the .ui files to Python code using the uic tool provides a more robust and maintainable solution for working with **Qt Designer**-generated UIs in Python applications.

Looking inside a .UI file

This .example ui file describes very a simple main window with a QLabel widget that displays the text "Hello, world!". The window is set to be 200 pixels wide and 150 pixels tall, and its title is set to "My Main Window". The window contains a single central widget, which is a **QWidget** layout containing a single **QLabel** widget. The file also includes an empty <resources> section and an empty <connections> section, which can be used to include external resources and connect signals and slots, respectively. I have saved the design as “helloworld.ui”

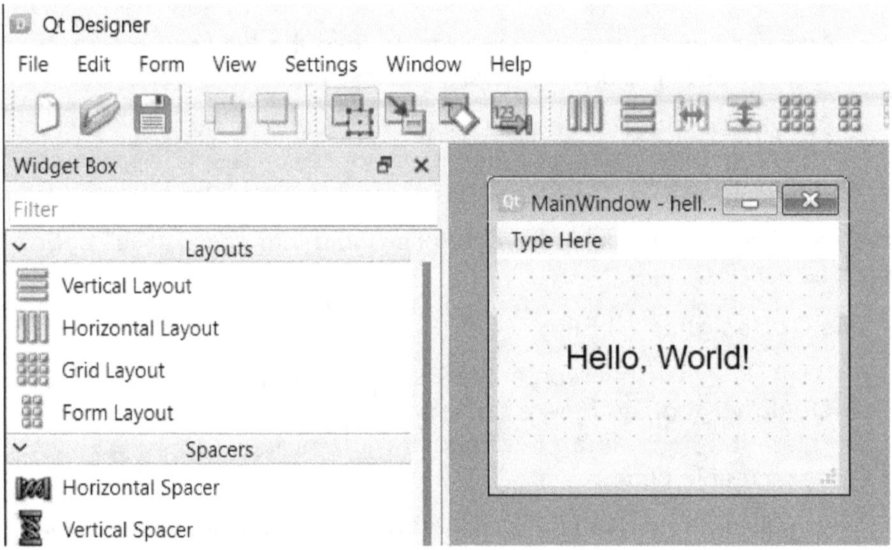

If we look inside “helloworld.ui” using Windows Notepad or similar we see that it is a text file containing the following XML:

```
<?xml version="1.0" encoding="UTF-8"?>
<ui version="4.0">
 <class>MainWindow</class>
 <widget class="QMainWindow" name="MainWindow">
  <property name="geometry">
   <rect>
    <x>0</x>
    <y>0</y>
    <width>200</width>
    <height>150</height>
   </rect>
  </property>
  <property name="minimumSize">
   <size>
    <width>200</width>
    <height>150</height>
   </size>
```

```
  </property>
  <property name="windowTitle">
   <string>MainWindow</string>
  </property>
  <widget class="QWidget" name="centralwidget">
   <widget class="QLabel" name="label">
    <property name="geometry">
     <rect>
      <x>40</x>
      <y>40</y>
      <width>121</width>
      <height>31</height>
     </rect>
    </property>
    <property name="font">
     <font>
      <family>Arial</family>
      <pointsize>14</pointsize>
     </font>
    </property>
    <property name="text">
     <string>Hello, World!</string>
    </property>
   </widget>
  </widget>
  <widget class="QMenuBar" name="menubar">
   <property name="geometry">
    <rect>
     <x>0</x>
     <y>0</y>
     <width>200</width>
     <height>22</height>
    </rect>
   </property>
  </widget>
  <widget class="QStatusBar" name="statusbar"/>
 </widget>
 <resources/>
 <connections/>
</ui>
```

How to use a Qt Designer UI File in Python

What next? Having created the GUI in **Qt Designer**, how is the resulting saved ***.UI** file used in Python? There are several options for using a **.ui** file created in **Qt Designer** in a Python program. Here are three common options:

1. Converting **.ui** file to **.py** file using the **pyuic6** tool: The **pyuic6** tool is a command-line utility that converts a **.ui** file to a Python module. This resulting Python module can be imported into your Python program and used to create the GUI or with the -X option can create executable code.
2. Using the **uic** module in Python to load the **.ui** file dynamically: The **uic** module provides a way to load a **.ui** file dynamically at runtime, without the need to convert it to a **.py** file. To use this approach, you need to import the uic module and call its **loadUi()** method, passing in the path to your **.ui** file and the object that you want to load the GUI into. This method has the advantage that if you subsequently edit the UI in **Qt Designer**, there is no need to then convert it again before it can be used.
3. Embedding the **.ui** file as a resource in the Python program: **PyQ**t supports embedding resource files in the Python program, which can include **.ui** files. To use this approach, you need to create a .qrc file that references your .ui file, and then compile the .qrc file into a Python module using the **pyrcc** tool. In **PyQt**, a **QRC** (Qt Resource Collection) file is an **XML** file that specifies a collection of binary or textual files and the resources they contain. These files can include icons, images, sounds, translation files, and other resources that may be required by a **PyQt** application.

We will look at each of these three options in turn:

(1) Converting .UI files to Python using the pyuic6 tool

To convert a .ui file to a .py file using pyuic, open a terminal window and navigate to the directory containing your .ui file. Convert the .ui file to a .py file: Use the **pyuic6** tool to convert your .ui file to a .py file

Once you have designed the interface, you will save your GUI design to a **.ui** (user interface) file. Before it can be used, the **.ui** file will need to be converted to a **.py** (Python) file that can be used in your application. This is done as follows:

pyuic6 -x interface_file.ui -o interface_file.py

where **pyuic6** has the following parameters:

inputfile: The path to the **.ui** file you want to convert to Python code.

-o <outputfile>: The optional output file path for the generated Python code. If not specified, the generated code will be written to stdout.

-x: Generate code for PyQt6's **QMainWindow** class instead of Python's **QWidget** class.

-p <module>: Add a from <module> import * statement at the beginning of the generated code. This is useful if you have custom widgets that need to be imported.

-i: Generate code for C++ enums as Python integer constants instead of string constants.

-d: Generate debug output.

-h, --help: Display help text and exit.

-v, --version: Display version information and exit.

Example Syntax:

pyuic6 inputfile.ui -o outputfile.py

pyuic6 helloworld.ui -o helloworld.py

which in this instance, converting the XML file (shown above) produces this helloworld.py Python file. Please note that this file is not in itself directly executable (see below) but can be imported (e.g **import helloworld.py**):

```
# Form implementation generated from reading ui file 'helloworld.ui'
#
# Created by: PyQt6 UI code generator 6.4.2
#
# WARNING: Any manual changes made to this file will be lost when pyuic6
is
# run again.  Do not edit this file unless you know what you are doing.


from PyQt6 import QtCore, QtGui, QtWidgets


class Ui_MainWindow(object):
    def setupUi(self, MainWindow):
        MainWindow.setObjectName("MainWindow")
        MainWindow.resize(200, 150)
        MainWindow.setMinimumSize(QtCore.QSize(200, 150))
        self.centralwidget = QtWidgets.QWidget(parent=MainWindow)
        self.centralwidget.setObjectName("centralwidget")
        self.label = QtWidgets.QLabel(parent=self.centralwidget)
        self.label.setGeometry(QtCore.QRect(40, 40, 121, 31))
        font = QtGui.QFont()
        font.setFamily("Arial")
        font.setPointSize(14)
        self.label.setFont(font)
        self.label.setObjectName("label")
        MainWindow.setCentralWidget(self.centralwidget)
        self.menubar = QtWidgets.QMenuBar(parent=MainWindow)
        self.menubar.setGeometry(QtCore.QRect(0, 0, 200, 22))
        self.menubar.setObjectName("menubar")
```

```
        MainWindow.setMenuBar(self.menubar)
        self.statusbar = QtWidgets.QStatusBar(parent=MainWindow)
        self.statusbar.setObjectName("statusbar")
        MainWindow.setStatusBar(self.statusbar)

        self.retranslateUi(MainWindow)
        QtCore.QMetaObject.connectSlotsByName(MainWindow)

    def retranslateUi(self, MainWindow):
        _translate = QtCore.QCoreApplication.translate
        MainWindow.setWindowTitle(_translate("MainWindow",
"MainWindow"))
        self.label.setText(_translate("MainWindow", "Hello, World!"))
```

If I instead ran

pyuic6 helloworld.ui -o helloworld.py -X

The **-X** creates an executable version of **helloworld.py**

Which as you can see below has a little extra code allowing it to be run with the command:

Python helloworld.py

The eXecutable code version of **helloworld.py**

```
# Form implementation generated from reading ui file 'helloworld.ui'
#
# Created by: PyQt6 UI code generator 6.4.2
#
# WARNING: Any manual changes made to this file will be lost when pyuic6
is
# run again.  Do not edit this file unless you know what you are doing.


from PyQt6 import QtCore, QtGui, QtWidgets


class Ui_MainWindow(object):
    def setupUi(self, MainWindow):
        MainWindow.setObjectName("MainWindow")
        MainWindow.resize(202, 150)
        MainWindow.setMinimumSize(QtCore.QSize(200, 150))
        self.centralwidget = QtWidgets.QWidget(parent=MainWindow)
```

```
        self.centralwidget.setObjectName("centralwidget")
        self.label = QtWidgets.QLabel(parent=self.centralwidget)
        self.label.setGeometry(QtCore.QRect(40, 10, 121, 31))
        font = QtGui.QFont()
        font.setFamily("Arial")
        font.setPointSize(14)
        self.label.setFont(font)
        self.label.setObjectName("label")
        self.pushButton = QtWidgets.QPushButton(parent=self.centralwidget)
        self.pushButton.setGeometry(QtCore.QRect(60, 70, 75, 24))
        self.pushButton.setObjectName("pushButton")
        MainWindow.setCentralWidget(self.centralwidget)
        self.menubar = QtWidgets.QMenuBar(parent=MainWindow)
        self.menubar.setGeometry(QtCore.QRect(0, 0, 202, 22))
        self.menubar.setObjectName("menubar")
        MainWindow.setMenuBar(self.menubar)
        self.statusbar = QtWidgets.QStatusBar(parent=MainWindow)
        self.statusbar.setObjectName("statusbar")
        MainWindow.setStatusBar(self.statusbar)

        self.retranslateUi(MainWindow)
        QtCore.QMetaObject.connectSlotsByName(MainWindow)

    def retranslateUi(self, MainWindow):
        _translate = QtCore.QCoreApplication.translate
        MainWindow.setWindowTitle(_translate("MainWindow",
"MainWindow"))
        self.label.setText(_translate("MainWindow", "Hello, World!"))
        self.pushButton.setText(_translate("MainWindow", "Push Me"))


if __name__ == "__main__":
    import sys
    app = QtWidgets.QApplication(sys.argv)
    MainWindow = QtWidgets.QMainWindow()
    ui = Ui_MainWindow()
    ui.setupUi(MainWindow)
    MainWindow.show()
    sys.exit(app.exec())
```

Outputs the GUI as designed in **Qt Designer**:

Of course, this code would still need work as it of course does not provide (for example) Pushbuttons that actually function. While you may find that this is a good starting point to check the appearance of your UI this is really as far as you should go. If you use this code as the basis of a project then you will be in trouble every time that you use **QT Designer** to update the UI (hence the warning in the code). In my opinion, method 2 (Using the uic module to load the .ui file dynamically as described below) is superior.

(2) Using the uic module to load the .ui file dynamically

Let me say straight off, in my opinion this is the easiest solution and is the one that I use. The reason is unlike the solution above that if you go back to the **Qt Designer** to make some adjustments to the UI you won't necessarily need to edit your Python code as the UI stays in the .ui file which is only loaded into Python at runtime. Many changes to the UI file (e.g. adjusting the layout, font sizes etc.) may not require any changes to the main Python code.

Here is an example data entry form that I have created in Qt Designer:

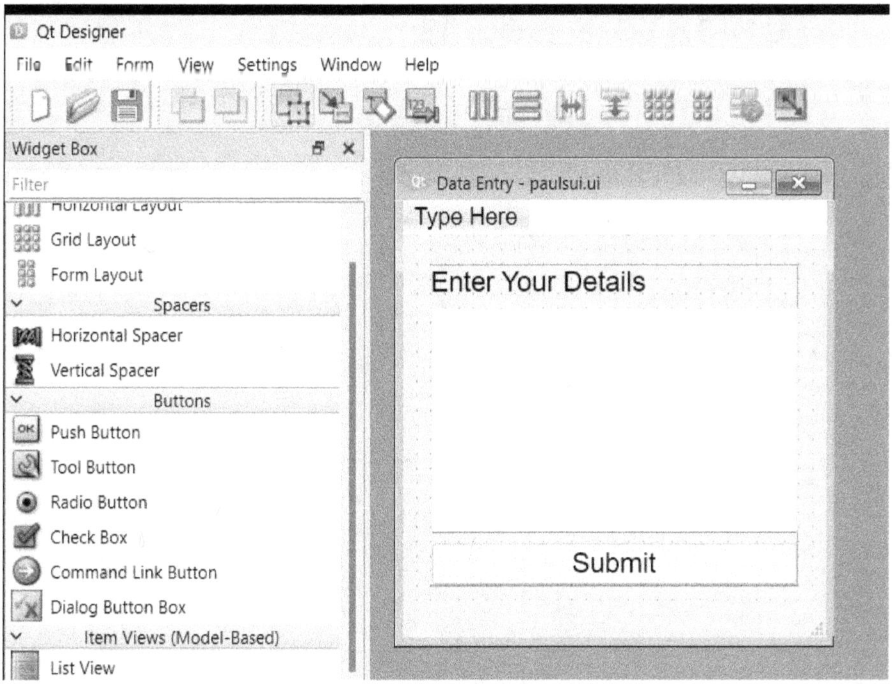

I've deliberately made this very small and simple.

The file is saved as **paulsui.ui**

With just a very few lines of code, Python loads my UI file and displays the Window. Note that you need to import from PyQt6.QtWidgets the Widgets that you have used and also (from PyQt6) the uic user interface converter:

```
from PyQt6.QtWidgets import QMainWindow, QApplication, QLabel,
QPushButton, QTextEdit
from PyQt6 import uic # user interface converter
import sys

app = QApplication([])
ui_file = r"c:\Users\paul_\paulsui.ui"
window = uic.loadUi(ui_file)
```

```
window.show()
app.exec()
```

Output – (I have entered some text into the blank form):

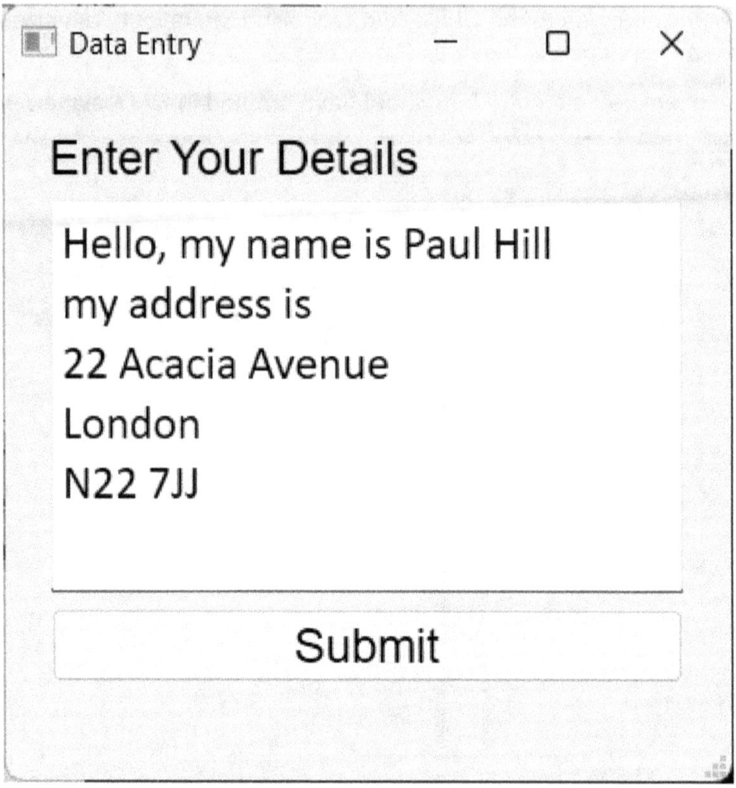

Of course, these few lines of code don't really do anything (yet) but it shows just how easy it is, how little Python code is required and how quickly you can make changes to the UI in **Qt Designer** and see what they look like on screen.

If you want to see how to activate the submit button to read the text there are a few additions required to the code:

```
from PyQt6.QtWidgets import QMainWindow, QApplication, QLabel,
QPushButton, QTextEdit
from PyQt6 import uic # user interface converter
import sys

app = QApplication([])
ui_file = r"c:\Users\paul_\paulsui.ui"
window = uic.loadUi(ui_file)

def submit_clicked():
```

```
    print(window.textEdit.toPlainText())

# Customise the user interface
window.setWindowTitle("My Window Title")
window.pushButton.clicked.connect(submit_clicked)

window.show()
app.exec()
```

Output:

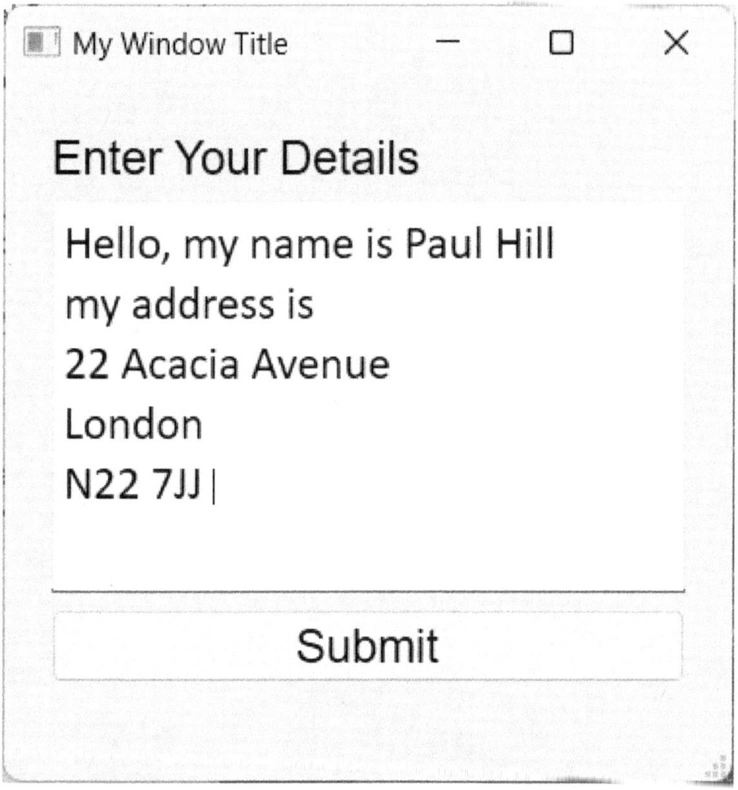

The changes are as follows:

Please note that we refer to both the push button and the text edit box in the code. These have the names that they were given in **Qt Designer**. I did not change these from the defaults so they are **pushButton** and **textEdit** respectively (like the Qt Widget names but without the initial Q and starting with a lower case letter).

We have defined a function called **submit_clicked** which will retrieve the text from the **textEdit** box and print it to the console/command prompt using **print(window.textEdit.toPlainText()).**

We have also used **window.pushButton.clicked.connect(submit_clicked)** to detect the button being clicked which calls the function mentioned.

Lastly, you may have noticed that the Window Title has changed. we have used **window.setWindowTitle("My Window Title")** simply to show that your Python code can overwrite settings that you have made in **Qt Designer** and saved in the **.UI** file.

I think that this demonstrated that this method is perhaps the easiest way to design a UI with **Qt Designer** and then use the file created directly in Python

(3) Using a Qt Resource Collection.

Qt Resource Collection (**QRC**) files are a way to bundle application resources, such as images, icons, fonts, translations, and other files, into a single file that can be easily distributed and accessed by Qt applications.

QRC files are an XML-based format that defines a list of resources that your application needs to use. The resources can be stored as raw binary data or compressed using the zlib compression algorithm. When you compile your application, the resources in the **QRC** file are compiled into the application binary and can be accessed at runtime using Qt's resource system.

QRC files simplify the process of managing and deploying application resources, as you can bundle all the required resources into a single file, rather than having to manage them separately. They also make it easy to distribute and install your application, as you only need to distribute a single binary file.

In Qt, you can access resources in a **QRC** file using the **QResource** class, which provides methods for loading and accessing resources from a **QRC** file. You can also use **Qt Designer** or **Qt Creator** to create and edit **QRC** files visually, making it easy to manage your application's resources.

The **pyrcc** tool is a command-line utility that is part of the PyQt toolkit for Python. It is used to compile Qt Resource Collection (**QRC**) files into Python modules that can be imported and used in a **PyQt** application.

You can store various types of resources in a Qt Resource Collection (**QRC**) file, including:

Images: PNG, JPEG, BMP, GIF, SVG, and other image formats.
Icons: Windows ICO, Apple ICNS, and other icon formats.
Fonts: TrueType (TTF) and OpenType (OTF) font files.
Translations: .qm files containing translations for your strings.
Text files: any text-based file format, such as XML, JSON, CSV, etc.
Audio and video files: MP3, WAV, OGG, etc.
Stylesheets: CSS files used to style your application's widgets.

Custom resources: any binary data that can be loaded and used by your application, such as custom file formats or compressed data.

You can include any type of resource in a **QRC** file that your application needs to use. When you compile your application, the resources in the **QRC** file will be compiled into your application's executable or library, making them easily accessible at runtime. This helps to simplify your application's deployment and ensure that all required resources are available on the target system.

You can create a Qt Resource Collection (**QRC**) file using the **Qt Creator** or **Qt Designer** tool, which are part of the Qt development framework.

Here are the steps to create a **QRC** file in Qt Creator:

- Open **Qt Creator** and create a new Qt Resource File project by selecting "File" -> "New File or Project" -> "Qt" -> "Qt Resource File" from the menu.

- Choose a name and location for your **QRC** file and click "Next".
- In the "Add Files" dialog, you can add the files and resources that you want to include in your **QRC** file. You can add files by clicking on the "Add" button and selecting the files from your file system, or you can drag and drop files into the dialog.
- Once you have added all the files you want to include in your **QRC** file, click "Finish" to create the **QRC** file.

Now you can edit the **QRC** file in **Qt Creator's** resource editor. You can add new files or remove existing files, and you can also set properties for each file, such as its name, alias, and compression settings.

Once you have finished editing the **QRC** file, save your changes and build your project. The resources in the **QRC** file will be compiled into your application and will be available at runtime.

Alternatively, you can create a **QRC** file manually using a text editor, by writing the XML code that defines the resources in the file. The XML format for a **QRC** file is simple and easy to learn, and you can find examples and documentation in the Qt documentation or online resources.

When a **QRC** file is compiled with **pyrcc**, it generates a Python module that contains the binary contents of all the resources specified in the QRC file. The module can then be imported into a **PyQt** application and used to access the resources directly, without the need to load them from disk or distribute them separately with the application.

To use **pyrcc**, you need to have **PyQt** installed on your system, and you need to open a terminal or command prompt window and navigate to the directory containing your **QRC** file. Then, you can run the following command to compile the **QRC** file into a Python module:

pyrcc6 -o my_resources_rc.py my_resources.qrc

This command tells **pyrcc** to compile the my_resources.qrc file into a Python module named my_resources.py. You can then import this module into your **PyQt** application and use it to access the resources contained within the **QRC** file. The **pyrcc** tool is a command-line utility that is part of the PyQt toolkit for Python. It is used to compile Qt Resource Collection (**QRC**) files into Python modules that can be imported and used in a **PyQt** application.

Qt Creator

Qt Creator is an integrated development environment (IDE) used for developing software applications that use the Qt framework. It is a cross-platform IDE that provides features such as code editing, debugging, testing, and project management tools for developing applications in C++, QML, and JavaScript. **Qt Creator** is primarily used for developing desktop applications and mobile applications that run on various operating systems such as Windows, macOS, Linux, Android, and iOS. Qt Creator also includes a visual editor for designing graphical user interfaces (GUIs) using the Qt Widgets and QML frameworks.

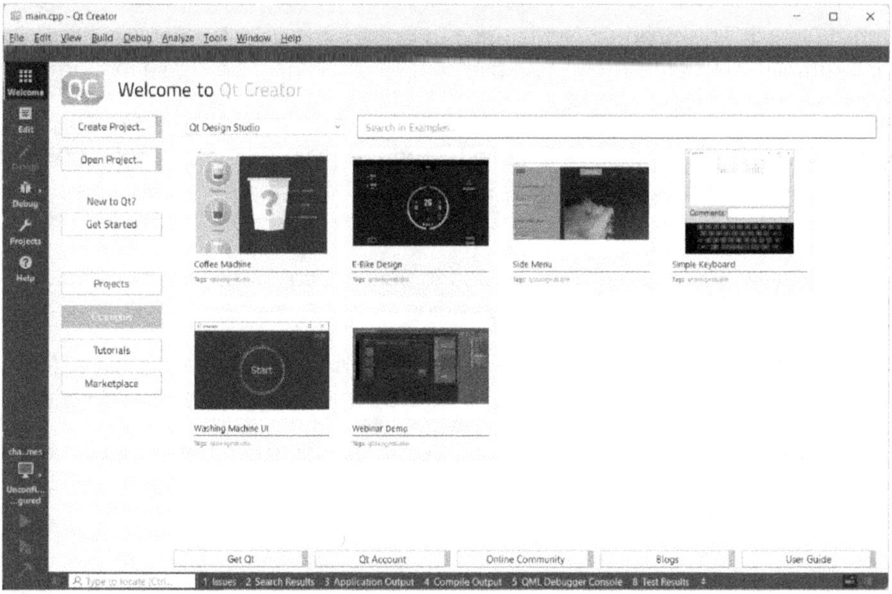

While **Qt Creator** is an excellent tool for developing Qt applications, it can be overwhelming and beyond the scope of an introduction to **PyQt6**.

While **Qt Creator** can be used to create GUI applications using **PyQt6,** it is not necessary for beginners to learn and use. The reason is that **Qt Creator** is designed for advanced users who want to build complex applications with many features, and it may have a steep learning curve for beginners. Instead, PyQt6 developers can use simple text editors or IDEs, such as Sublime Text, Visual Studio Code or PyCharm, to write and edit their code.

User Dialogs

PyQt6 provides a set of dialog classes that can be used to display various types of dialog boxes in a graphical user interface (GUI) application. Dialogs are used to prompt the user for input, display information, or confirm an action.

Here are some of the most commonly used PyQt6 dialog classes:

QMessageBox: This dialog class is used to display a message to the user, such as an error message or a confirmation message. It has different types of buttons that can be added to it, such as "Ok", "Yes", "No", and "Cancel".

QInputDialog: This dialog class is used to prompt the user for input, such as a string, number, or password. It has different types of input fields, such as a line edit, a combo box, or a spin box.

QFileDialog: This dialog class is used to open or save files. It has different modes that can be set, such as "Open" or "Save", and it can filter the types of files that can be selected.

QColorDialog: This dialog class is used to select a colour. It displays a colour wheel and allows the user to select a colour.

QFontDialog: This dialog class is used to select a font. It displays a list of fonts and allows the user to select a font and its properties, such as size and style.

QProgressDialog: This dialog class is used to display a progress bar or a busy indicator. It can be used to show the progress of a long-running operation, such as a file download or a data processing task.

For detail on each and examples of their use, see the section on each in the alphabetical section on Widgets & Dialogs.

These dialog classes provide a simple and consistent way to display dialogs in a PyQt6 application. They are easy to use and can be customised to fit the specific needs of an application.

Styles and Themes in PyQt6

A theme in **PyQt6** refers to a collection of styles and settings that define the overall look and feel of the application's user interface. A theme encompasses multiple visual elements, such as colours, fonts, and layout, and defines the overall visual style of the application. **PyQt6** provides several built-in themes that you can use to change the appearance of your application, such as Fusion, Windows, and Macintosh.

A style in **PyQt6** refers to the specific appearance of a single UI element, such as a button, label, or text box. A style defines the visual properties of the element, such as its colour, size, and shape. **PyQt6** provides several built-in styles that you can use to customise the appearance of individual UI elements, such as Windows, Macintosh, Plastique, and CleanLooks.

PyQt6 provides a default style known as the "Fusion" style, which is a modern, flat, and minimalist style that works well on all platforms. However, developers can also choose from a variety of other built-in styles such as "Windows", "Macintosh", "Plastique", and "Cleanlooks", among others dependant on the Operating system in use.

To check which Styles are available on your system by default enter:

```
from PyQt6.QtWidgets import QStyleFactory
print(QStyleFactory.keys())
```

and the output is a list. On my Windows11 system:

['windowsvista', 'Windows', 'Fusion']

In addition to the built-in styles, **PyQt6** allows developers to create custom styles by subclassing the **QStyle** class. This enables developers to tailor the look and feel of their applications to match their specific requirements.

Themes in **PyQt6** are a collection of styles that can be used to change the overall appearance of an application. **PyQt6** includes several built-in themes, such as "Dark", "Light", and "Classic", which change the colour schemes and visual properties of the underlying styles.

Developers can also create custom themes by combining and modifying existing styles. This can be useful when creating applications with specific branding requirements or when trying to create a unique visual identity for an application.

Changing Style

To select a style in **PyQt6**, you can use the **QApplication.setStyle()** method to set the default style for your application or the **QWidget.setStyle()** method to set the style for individual widgets.

The styles available will depend on your Operating System. Some of the available built-in styles in **PyQt6** include:

- "Windows": The Windows style

- "WindowsXP": The Windows XP style
- "WindowsVista": The Windows Vista style
- "Windows7": The Windows 7 style
- "Fusion": The Fusion style (default on many platforms)
- "Macintosh": The Macintosh style
- "Breeze": The Breeze style (default on KDE Plasma)
- "GTK+": The GTK+ style (default on GNOME)
- "QtCurve": The QtCurve style
- "Plastique": The Plastique style

For example, to set the Fusion style as the default style for your application, you can use the following code:

```
from PyQt6.QtWidgets import QApplication

app = QApplication([])
app.setStyle("fusion")
```

In addition to setting the default style for your application, you can also set the style for individual widgets by calling the **QWidget.setStyle()** method. This can be useful if you want to use a different style for a specific widget or group of widgets.

Example:

```
widget = QWidget()
widget.setStyle("fusion")
```

Creating Custom Themes with QPalette

In **PyQt6**, you can change the theme of your application by setting the palette of the application or individual widgets. The palette defines the colours and other visual properties of the UI elements in your application.

To change the theme of your application, you can use the **QPalette** class to create a new palette with different colours and properties. You can then set this palette as the default palette for your application using the **QApplication.setPalette()** method.

For example, to set a dark theme for your application, you can create a QPalette object with dark colours and set it as the default palette using the following code:

```
from PyQt6.QtWidgets import QApplication
from PyQt6.QtGui import QPalette, QColor

app = QApplication([])

# Create a new palette with dark colours
palette = QPalette()
palette.setColor(QPalette.ColorRole.Window, QColor(53, 53, 53))
palette.setColor(QPalette.ColorRole.WindowText, QColor(255, 255, 255))
palette.setColor(QPalette.ColorRole.Base, QColor(25, 25, 25))
palette.setColor(QPalette.ColorRole.AlternateBase, QColor(53, 53, 53))
palette.setColor(QPalette.ColorRole.ToolTipBase, QColor(255, 255, 255))
palette.setColor(QPalette.ColorRole.ToolTipText, QColor(255, 255, 255))
palette.setColor(QPalette.ColorRole.Text, QColor(255, 255, 255))
palette.setColor(QPalette.ColorRole.Button, QColor(53, 53, 53))
palette.setColor(QPalette.ColorRole.ButtonText, QColor(255, 255, 255))
palette.setColor(QPalette.ColorRole.BrightText, QColor(255, 0, 0))
palette.setColor(QPalette.ColorRole.Highlight, QColor(142, 45, 197))
palette.setColor(QPalette.ColorRole.HighlightedText, QColor(255, 255,
255))

# Set the new palette as the default palette for the application
app.setPalette(palette)
```

This will set the dark theme as the default theme for your application.

Alternatively, you can set the palette for individual widgets by calling the QWidget.setPalette() method.

The setStyleSheet Method

The **setStyleSheet()** method in PyQt allows you to apply CSS-like style sheets to Qt widgets, such as QLabels, to customise their appearance.

Here are some of the style properties that you can set using **setStyleSheet():**

background-color	sets the background colour of the widget
border	sets the border properties of the widget (e.g. width, style, colour)
color	sets the text colour of the widget
font-family	sets the font family used for the widget's text
font-size	sets the font size used for the widget's text
padding	sets the padding around the content of the widget
margin	sets the margin around the outside of the widget
text-align	sets the horizontal alignment of the widget's text (e.g. left, center, right)

Here are some examples of what you can do with **setStyleSheet():**

Set the background colour of a QLabel:

label.setStyleSheet("background-color: yellow;")

Set the font family and size of a QLabel:

label.setStyleSheet("font-family: Arial; font-size: 16px;")

Set the text colour of a QPushButton when it's in a disabled state:

button.setStyleSheet("color: gray;" "background-color: lightgray;" "border-color: gray;")

Create a custom look for a QSlider:

slider.setStyleSheet("QSlider::groove:horizontal { background: white; height: 6px; border-radius: 3px; }" "QSlider::handle:horizontal { background: qlineargradient(x1:0, y1:0, x2:1, y2:1, stop:0 #eee, stop:1 #ccc); width: 20px; margin: -6px 0; border-radius: 10px; }")

In addition to setting style properties like colour, background-colour, font-family, and font-size, you can also use **setStyleSheet()** to set other style-related properties, such as border, padding, margin, text-align, box-shadow, and many others. You can also use CSS selectors to target specific elements or states of a widget, such as :hover, :pressed, :checked, and so on. The possibilities are nearly endless, and **setStyleSheet()** provides a powerful way to customise the appearance of Qt widgets in PyQt.

Importing and using 3rd Party Themes

There are a number of 3rd party Themes available including **qdarkstyle** and **qtmodern** which can be installed. These need to be installed before they can be used.

Examplo **qdarkstyle** which can then be imported and used as follows:

pip install qdarkstyle

```
from PyQt6.QtWidgets import QApplication
import qdarkstyle

# Create a QApplication instance
app = QApplication([])

# Set the application style to the QDarkStyle theme
app.setStyleSheet(qdarkstyle.load_stylesheet())
```

Another example :

pip install qtmodern

used as follows:

```
import qtmodern.styles
import qtmodern.windows

# Create a QApplication instance
app = QApplication([])

# Set the application style to Light or Dark
qtmodern.styles.light(app) # or dark
```

Working with Files and Directories

PyQt6 provides a variety of modules and classes for working with files and directories, such as **QFile**, **QDir**, and **QFileDialog**.

These modules and classes can be used to list the contents of a directory, filter files based on their attributes (such as file extension, modification date, etc.), and perform other file-related operations.

QFile

QFile is a class that provides an interface for reading from and writing to files. It is a subclass of the **QIODevice** class and inherits its methods for reading and writing data.

The **QFile** class provides methods for opening and closing files, reading and writing data to files, and querying file information such as the file size and permissions. It also provides methods for working with file paths, such as converting between relative and absolute paths.

Here are some common methods of **QFile**:

open(mode)	Opens the file with the specified mode (e.g. QIODevice.ReadOnly, QIODevice.WriteOnly, QIODevice.ReadWrite).
close()	Closes the file.
read(size)	Reads and returns the specified number of bytes from the file.
write(data)	Writes the specified data to the file.
seek(pos)	Sets the file position indicator to the specified position.
size()	Returns the size of the file in bytes.
fileName()	Returns the name of the file.
exists()	Returns True if the file exists, False otherwise.

Here's a very simple example of using **QFile** to read and output the contents of a file. The file is opened in read-only mode and a **QTextStream** is used to read the file's contents. The file is then closed and its contents are printed to the console.

```
from PyQt6.QtCore import QFile

file = QFile('example.txt')
if file.open(QFile.ReadOnly | QFile.Text):
    stream = QTextStream(file)
    content = stream.readAll()
    file.close()
    print(content)
```

QDir

QDir provides access to directory structures and their contents. It is commonly used for file management tasks, such as locating files and directories and managing file paths.

Features of **QDir** include the ability to navigate directories using both absolute and relative paths, to filter files and directories based on various criteria, and to sort file and directory lists by name, size, and other attributes. **QDir** also provides methods for creating, renaming, copying, and deleting files and directories. The QDir class also provides methods for working with file system paths, such as **absolutePath(), canonicalPath(),** and **isRelative().** Additionally, it provides methods for converting between **QDir** and **QString** representations of file system paths.

One of the advantages of using **QDir** is that it is cross-platform, meaning that it can be used on different operating systems without modification. This allows you to write portable code that works on Windows, macOS, Linux, and other platforms supported by Qt.

Syntax:

 # create a QDir object for the current working directory

my_dir = QDir()

Methods:

Some useful methods for working with directories, include:

entryList()	returns a list of files and directories in a directory.
mkdir()	creates a new directory.
rmdir()	removes a directory.
exists()	checks whether a directory exists.
cd()	changes the current directory.
path()	returns the path of the directory.

Example:

```
# create a QDir object for the current working directory
dir = QDir()

# list the contents of the directory
dirList = dir.entryList()

# create a new directory
dir.mkdir("new_dir")

# check if a directory exists
if dir.exists("existing_dir"):
    print("The directory exists.")

# navigate to a subdirectory
dir.cd("existing_dir/subdir")

# get the current directory path
currentPath = dir.path()
```

QFileDialog

QFileDialog is a class that provides a dialog for file selection and saving. It allows the user to browse through the file system and select a file or specify a file name for saving.

QFileDialog provides a variety of options for filtering and selecting files, including filtering by file type, displaying file details such as size and modification date, and selecting multiple files.

Syntax:

dialog = QFileDialog()

(see example below)

Here are some common methods of **QFileDialog**:

getOpenFileName(parent, caption, directory, filter, options)	Opens a dialog for selecting a single file to open. Returns a tuple containing the selected file name and the selected file type.
getOpenFileNames(parent, caption, directory, filter, options)	Opens a dialog for selecting multiple files to open. Returns a list of selected file names.
getSaveFileName(parent, caption, directory, filter, options)	Opens a dialog for selecting a file name to save. Returns the selected file name.
setFileMode(mode)	Sets the file selection mode (e.g. QFileDialog.AnyFile, QFileDialog.ExistingFile, QFileDialog.Directory, QFileDialog.ExistingFiles).
setNameFilter(filter)	Sets a file name filter (e.g. "Text files (*.txt)").
setViewMode(mode)	Sets the view mode for the file dialog (e.g. QFileDialog.List, QFileDialog.Details).
setDefaultSuffix(suffix)	Sets the default file name suffix.

Here's a simple example of using **QFileDialog** to select and open a file. The files that can be selected are filtered to Python files (*.py)

```
from PyQt6.QtWidgets import QApplication, QFileDialog

app = QApplication([])
dialog = QFileDialog()
dialog.setFileMode(QFileDialog.FileMode.ExistingFile)
dialog.setNameFilter("Python files (*.py)")
if dialog.exec():
    selected_file = dialog.selectedFiles()[0]
    with open(selected_file, "r") as file:
        content = file.read()
        print(content)
```

Output:

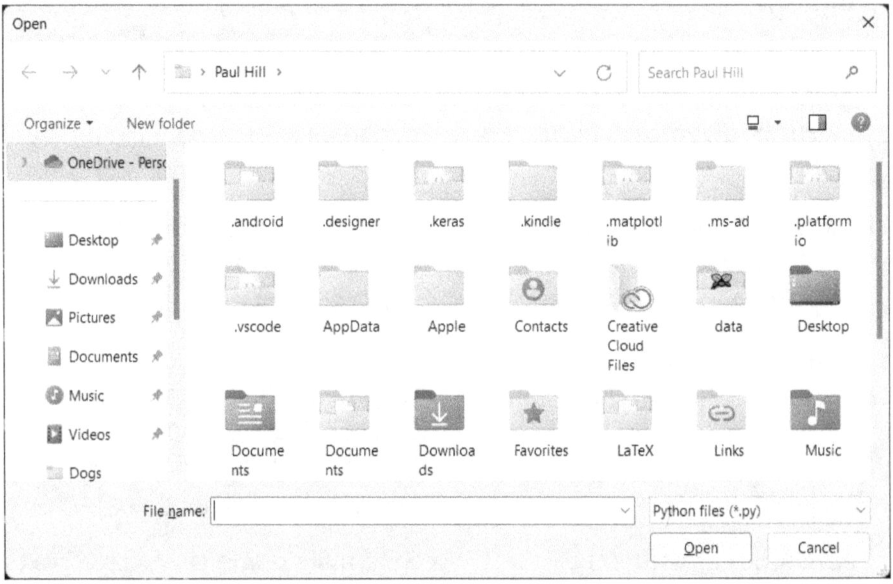

You will see (bottom right) that the files shown are filtered to Python *.py files.

(And the content of the selected file is then output to the console/command prompt).

WebEngine

PyQt6-WebEngine is a Python package that provides a set of bindings for the QtWebEngine module in the Qt framework, allowing developers to create web-based user interfaces using Python and **PyQt6**.

The **QtWebEngine** module provides a web engine based on the Chromium browser engine, allowing developers to create modern, feature-rich web applications using a range of web technologies such as HTML, CSS, and JavaScript.

PyQt6-WebEngine includes a set of Python classes that provide access to the functionality of the QtWebEngine module, making it easy to create and manipulate web content within **PyQt6** applications. This includes classes for creating web views, loading web content, and interacting with web pages.

Using **PyQt6**-WebEngine, developers can create powerful, cross-platform applications that combine the functionality of the web with the power and flexibility of Python and **PyQt6**. It is particularly useful for creating applications that require rich and interactive user interfaces, such as multimedia applications, games, and productivity tools.

Installing:

pip install PyQt6-WebEngine

Some of the methods used with **QtWebEngine** include:

QWebEngineView.load(url) Loads the web page at the specified URL into the view.

QWebEngineView.setHtml(html, baseUrl) Loads the specified HTML content into the view.

QWebEngineView.page() Returns the QWebEnginePage object associated with the view.

QWebEnginePage.runJavaScript(script, callback) Executes the specified JavaScript code on the current web page and calls the specified callback function with the result.

QWebEnginePage.settings() Returns the QWebEngineSettings object for the current web page.

QWebEnginePage.scroll(dx, dy) Scrolls the web page by the specified amount.

Example

```
from PyQt6.QtCore import QUrl
from PyQt6.QtWebEngineWidgets import QWebEngineView
from PyQt6.QtWidgets import QApplication, QMainWindow

class MapWidget(QMainWindow):
    def __init__(self):
        super().__init__()
        self.setWindowTitle("Map Widget")
        # Create a QWebEngineView widget
        self.webview = QWebEngineView(self)
        self.setCentralWidget(self.webview)
        # Load the map from a URL
        url = QUrl("https://www.openstreetmap.org")
        self.webview.load(url)

if __name__ == '__main__':
    app = QApplication([])
    window = MapWidget()
    window.show()
    app.exec()
```

Output:

PyQT6 Widgets & Dialogs (alphabetical)

There are many PyQT6 widgets available – over 100 - that can be used to create graphical user interfaces. Many of them are listed below. As this book is an introduction to PyQt6 I won't cover them all in detail however many of the most commonly used will be discussed below complete with syntax, options and simple examples of their use.

QAbstractButton
QAbstractGraphicsShapeItem
QAbstractItemDelegate
QAbstractItemView
QAction
QActionGroup
QApplication
QBoxLayout
QButtonGroup
QPushButton
QCalendarWidget
QCheckBox
QColorDialog
QColumnView
QComboBox
QCommandLinkButton
QCompleter
QDataWidgetMapper
QDateEdit
QDateTimeEdit
QDesktopWidget
QDialog
QDialogButtonBox
QDirModel
QDockWidget
QDoubleSpinBox
QErrorMessage
QFileDialog
QFileIconProvider
QFileSystemModel
QFontComboBox
QFontDialog
QFormLayout
QGraphicsEllipseItem
QGraphicsItem
QGraphicsLineItem
QGraphicsPathItem
QGraphicsPixmapItem
QGraphicsPolygonItem
QGraphicsRectItem
QGraphicsScene
QGraphicsSceneContextMenuEvent
QGraphicsSceneDragDropEvent
QGraphicsSceneEvent
QGraphicsSceneHelpEvent
QGraphicsSceneHoverEvent
QGraphicsSceneMouseEvent
QGraphicsSceneMoveEvent
QGraphicsSceneResizeEvent
QGraphicsSceneWheelEvent
QGraphicsSimpleTextItem
QGraphicsTextItem
QGraphicsView
QGridLayout
QGroupBox
QHeaderView
QHelpEvent
QInputDialog
QItemDelegate
QItemEditorFactory
QItemSelectionModel
QKeyEventTransition

QKeySequenceEdit	QLCDNumber
QLabel	QLayout
QLayoutItem	QLineEdit
QListWidget	QListWidgetItem
QMainWindow	QMenu
QMenuBar	QMessageBox
QMouseEventTransition	QMotifStyle
QMovie	QPageSetupDialog
QPanGesture	QPainter
QPainterPath	QPalette
QPen	QPicture
QPixmap	QPlainTextEdit
QProgressBar	QProgressDialog
QPushButton	QRadioButton
QRubberBand	QScrollArea
QScrollBar	QShortcut
QSizeGrip	QSlider
QSortFilterProxyModel	QSound
QSpinBox	QSplashScreen
QSplitter	QStackedLayout
QStackedWidget	QStatusBar
QStyle	QStyledItemDelegate
QSvgWidget	QSwipeGesture
QSystemTrayIcon	QTabBar
QTabletEvent	QTableView
QTableWidget	QTableWidgetItem
QTabWidget	QTextBrowser
QTextCharFormat	QTextCursor
QTextEdit	QTextFormat
QTextFrame	QTextImageFormat
QTextListFormat	QTextObject
QTextOption	QTextTableFormat
QToolBar	QToolBox
QToolButton	QToolTip

For more detailed information including syntax, options and example for the most commonly used PyQt6 widgets, please see below.

QCalendarWidget

The calendar widget is a graphical user interface element that displays a calendar to the user and allows the user to select a date from the displayed calendar.

Syntax:

my_calendar = QCalendarWidget(parent)

The **QCalendarWidget** provides several options to customise the appearance and behaviour of the calendar widget in PyQt6, you can set the minimum and maximum dates that can be displayed in the calendar widget by using the **setMinimumDate()** and **setMaximumDate()** methods, respectively:

my_calendar.setMinimumDate(QDate(2021, 1, 1))

my_calendar.setMaximumDate(QDate(2023, 12, 31))

you can set the first day of the week for the calendar by using the **setFirstDayOfWeek()** method:

my_calendar.setFirstDayOfWeek(Qt.DayOfWeek.Monday)

Qt.DayOfWeek specifies the days of the week, which can be used to set the first day of the week to Monday, Tuesday, Wednesday, Thursday, Friday, Saturday, or Sunday.

Finally, you can set whether the calendar widget displays a grid by using the **setGridVisible()** method:

my_calendar.setGridVisible(True)

This method takes a boolean value to specify whether the grid should be visible or not.

Example:

```
import sys
from PyQt6.QtWidgets import QApplication, QWidget, QCalendarWidget,
QVBoxLayout, QLabel

app = QApplication(sys.argv)

window = QWidget()  # Create a new QWidget
window.setWindowTitle('Calendar Widget')
window.setGeometry(300, 300, 350, 300)

# Create a calendar widget and add it to the layout
cal = QCalendarWidget(window)
cal.setGridVisible(True)

# Create a label to display the selected date
```

```
lbl = QLabel(window)
date = cal.selectedDate()
lbl.setText(date.toString())

# Connect the selectionChanged signal to a function that updates the label
def updateLabel():
    date = cal.selectedDate()
    lbl.setText(date.toString())

cal.selectionChanged.connect(updateLabel)

# Create a vertical layout and add the widgets to it
vbox = QVBoxLayout()
vbox.addWidget(cal)
vbox.addWidget(lbl)

# Set the layout for the main window
window.setLayout(vbox)

# Show the main window and run the event loop
window.show()
sys.exit(app.exec())
```

Output:

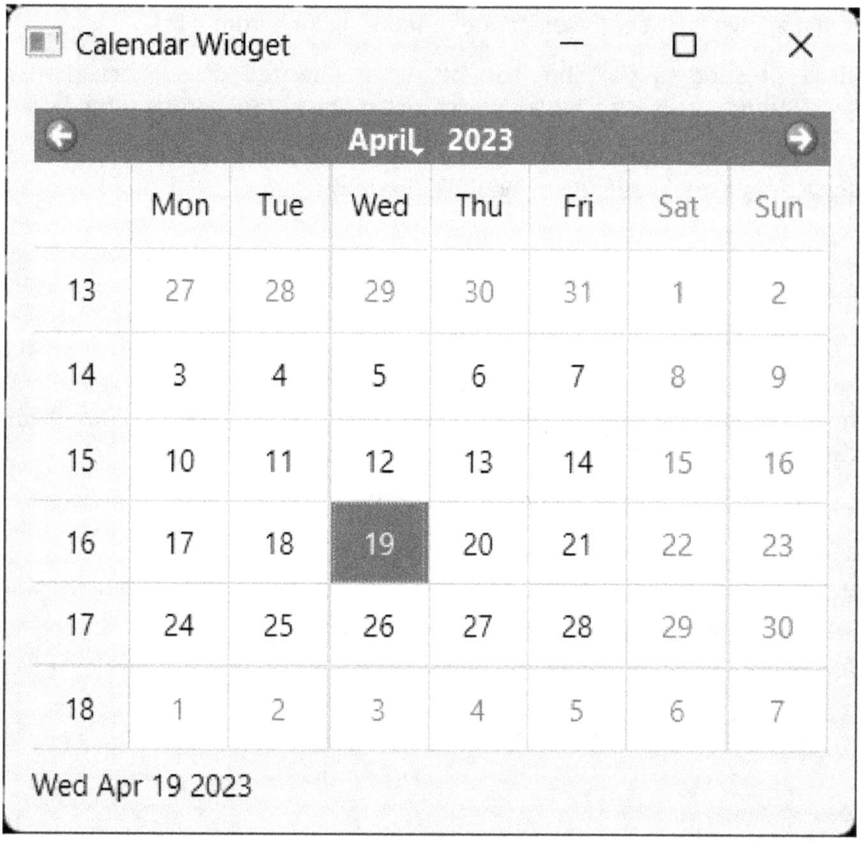
Calendar Widget
April 2023
Mon
Tue
Wed
Thu
Fri
Sat
Sun
13 27 28 29 30 31 1 2
14 3 4 5 6 7 8 9
15 10 11 12 13 14 15 16
16 17 18 19 20 21 22 23
17 24 25 26 27 28 29 30
18 1 2 3 4 5 6 7
Wed Apr 19 2023

QCheckBox

A widget that allows the user to select one or more options from a list.

QCheckBox presents a box that can be either checked or unchecked. It is commonly used to represent a binary choice or an option that can be turned on or off.

In **PyQt6, QCheckBox** is defined in the **QtWidgets** module.

Syntax:

 # create a QCheckBox widget

my_checkbox = QCheckBox('text', parent)

When the user interacts with the **QCheckBox**, it emits a stateChanged signal. You can connect to this signal to perform some action when the state of the QCheckBox changes. E.g.:

my_checkbox.stateChanged.connect(function)

Here's an example of how to create a **QCheckBox** widget:

```
import sys
from PyQt6.QtWidgets import QApplication, QDialog, QCheckBox,
QVBoxLayout

app = QApplication(sys.argv)

# Create a dialog window
dialog = QDialog()
dialog.setWindowTitle('QCheckBox Example')
dialog.setGeometry(300, 300, 250, 150)

# Create a QCheckBox widget
cb = QCheckBox('Show title', dialog)

# Create a vertical layout and add the checkbox to it
vert_box = QVBoxLayout()
vert_box.addWidget(cb)

dialog.setLayout(vert_box)

# Define a function to be called when the checkbox state changes
def changeTitle(state):
    if state == 2:
        dialog.setWindowTitle('QCheckBox Example - Title Shown')
    else:
```

```
    dialog.setWindowTitle('QCheckBox Example')

# Connect the stateChanged signal of the checkbox to the changeTitle
function
cb.stateChanged.connect(changeTitle)

# Show the dialog window
dialog.show()

sys.exit(app.exec())
```

Output:

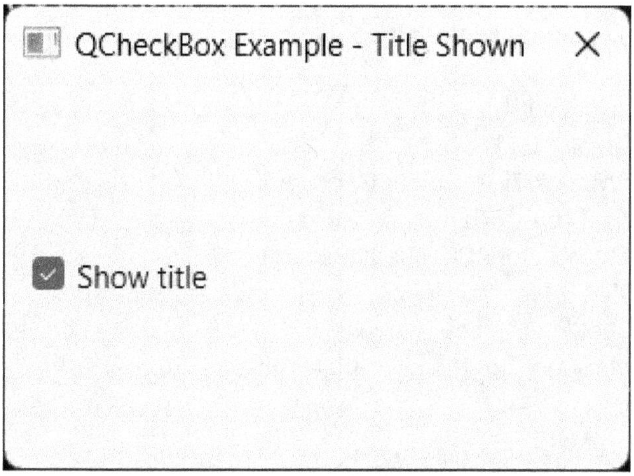

Note how the title changes depending on whether the “Show title” checkbox is selected or not.

QColorDialog

QColorDialog allows the user to select a colour from a colour wheel or by entering its RGB or HSV values. The selected colour can then be used to set the background or foreground colour of a widget, or to draw graphics in a **QPainter** object.

In PyQt, **QColorDialog** can be accessed through the **QColorDialog** class. To display the colour dialog, you can call the static function **getColor()** of the **QColorDialog** class, which returns the selected colour as a **QColor** object.

The **QColorDialog** class also provides a set of static functions for creating colour dialogs with different options, such as allowing the user to select a custom colour, or specifying the initial colour of the dialog.

Example (a slight variation on my Signals and Slots example):

```
from PyQt6.QtWidgets import *

app = QApplication([])
window = QMainWindow()
window.setWindowTitle('Colour Chooser')
window.resize(450, 150)
button = QPushButton('Choose a colour!')
button.setStyleSheet("font-family: Arial; font-size: 20px;")
label = QLabel('This is your colour')
label.setStyleSheet("font-family: Arial; font-size: 20px;")

def update_label():
    colour = QColorDialog.getColor()
    if colour.isValid():
        label.setStyleSheet("font-family: Arial; font-size: 20px; color: " +
colour.name() + ";")

button.clicked.connect(update_label)

layout = QHBoxLayout() # Horizontal Row

layout.addWidget(button)
layout.addWidget(label)

central_widget = QWidget()
central_widget.setLayout(layout)
window.setCentralWidget(central_widget)

window.show()
```

```
app.exec()
```

Output (In this case the chosen colour is red:

QComboBox

QComboBox is a widget that provides a drop-down menu with a list of items for the user to select from. It inherits the QAbstractItemView and QWidget classes.

Syntax

mycombobox = QComboBox(parent)

Some commonly used methods for **QComboBox**:

setGeometry(x, y, w, h)	Sets the position and size of the combo box on the screen. The method takes four arguments: x, y, width, and height.
addItem(text str, userData Any = None)	Adds an item to the end of the combo box with the given text.
addItems(items Iterable[str])	Adds multiple items to the end of the combo box.
clear()	Removes all items from the combo box.
count() -> int	Returns the number of items in the combo box.
currentIndex() -> int	Returns the index of the currently selected item.
currentText() -> str	Returns the text of the currently selected item.
insertItem(index int, text str, userData Any = None)	Inserts an item at the given index with the given text and optional user data.
insertItems(index int, items Iterable[str])	Inserts multiple items at the given index.
removeItem(index int)	Removes the item at the given index.
setItemText(index int, text str)	Sets the text of the item at the given index.
setEditable(editable bool)	Sets whether the combo box is editable or not.
setMinimumContentsLength(characters int)	Sets the minimum number of visible characters in the combo box.

setModel(model QAbstractItemModel)	Sets the model for the combo box.
setView(view QAbstractItemView)	Sets the view for the combo box.

Example:

```
from PyQt6.QtWidgets import QApplication, QWidget, QComboBox,
QVBoxLayout
import sys

app = QApplication(sys.argv)

# create a QWidget window
window = QWidget()
window.setWindowTitle('QComboBox Example')
window.setGeometry(300, 300, 300, 150)

# create a QComboBox widget and add some items to it
combo_box = QComboBox(window)
combo_box.addItem('Smarties')
combo_box.addItem('Minstrels')
combo_box.addItem('M&Ms')

# create a QVBoxLayout and add the QComboBox to it
vbox = QVBoxLayout()
vbox.addWidget(combo_box)

window.setLayout(vbox) # set the layout of the window

window.show() # show the window

# connect the activated signal to a slot function
def combo_box_activated(index):
    print('Selected item:', combo_box.itemText(index))

combo_box.activated.connect(combo_box_activated)

sys.exit(app.exec())
```

Output:

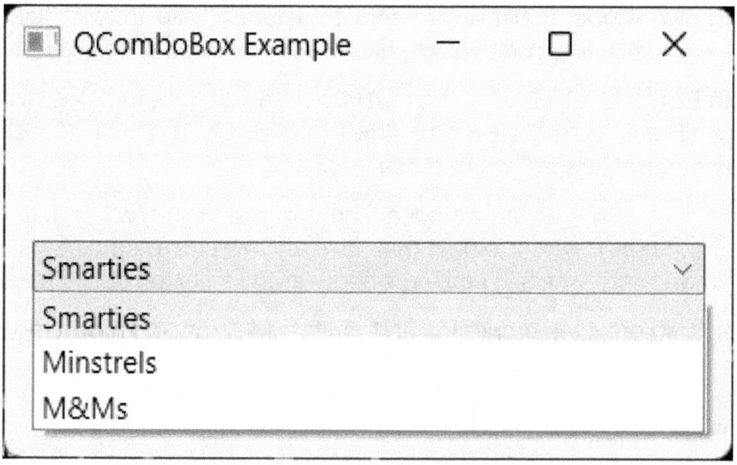

QDateEdit

QDateEdit is a widget that allows users to select a date from a calendar or by entering it manually. It provides a graphical user interface for editing dates.

The **QDateEdit** widget inherits from **QDateTimeEdit** (*see next*), which provides the ability to edit both dates and times. However, by default, **QDateEdit** is configured to only allow editing of dates.

QDateEdit provides various methods and signals to interact with the selected date, such as **date(),** which returns the currently selected date as a **QDate** object, and **dateChanged(),** which is emitted whenever the selected date is changed.

QDateEdit also provides properties and methods to customise its appearance and behavior, such as **setDisplayFormat(),** which allows you to specify the format used to display the selected date, and **setMinimumDate()** and **setMaximumDate(),** which allow you to set the minimum and maximum selectable dates.

Syntax:

date_edit = QDateEdit(parent)

date_edit.setDate(QDate.currentDate())

date_edit.setCalendarPopup(True)

Methods:

date()	returns the currently selected date as a QDate object.
setDate(QDate)	sets the currently selected date to the specified QDate object.
setCalendarPopup(bool)	enables or disables the calendar popup that allows users to select a date visually.
setDisplayFormat(str)	sets the format used to display the selected date.
setMinimumDate(QDate)	sets the minimum selectable date to the specified QDate object.
setMaximumDate(QDate)	sets the maximum selectable date to the specified QDate object.
setCalendarWidget(QWidget)	sets the widget used to display the calendar when the calendar popup is enabled.

setDateRange(QDate, QDate)	sets the minimum and maximum selectable dates to the specified QDate objects.

Example:

```
from PyQt6.QtWidgets import QApplication, QWidget, QVBoxLayout,
QDateEdit
from PyQt6.QtCore import QDate
import sys

app = QApplication(sys.argv)

window = QWidget()
window.setWindowTitle('QDateEdit Example')
window.setGeometry(300, 300, 300, 200)

date_edit = QDateEdit(window)
date_edit.setDate(QDate.currentDate())
date_edit.setCalendarPopup(True)

vbox = QVBoxLayout()
vbox.addWidget(date_edit)

window.setLayout(vbox)
window.show()

def date_changed(date):
    print('Selected date:', date.toString())

date_edit.dateChanged.connect(date_changed)

sys.exit(app.exec())
```

Output:

The Selected date is also output to the console / command prompt:

Selected date: Wed Mar 15 2023

QDateTimeEdit

QDateTimeEdit is a widget that allows users to select a date and time from a calendar and a time editor or by entering them manually. It provides a graphical user interface for editing dates and times.

QDateTimeEdit inherits from **QAbstractSpinBox** and provides a flexible and customisable user interface for editing date and time values.

QDateTimeEdit provides various methods and signals to interact with the selected date and time, such as **dateTime(),** which returns the currently selected date and time as a **QDateTime** object, and **dateTimeChanged(),** which is emitted whenever the selected date and time is changed.

QDateTimeEdit also provides properties and methods to customise its appearance and behavior, such as **setDisplayFormat(),** which allows you to specify the format used to display the selected date and time, and **setMinimumDateTime()** and **setMaximumDateTime(),** which allow you to set the minimum and maximum selectable date and time values.

Syntax:

my_datetime = QDateTimeEdit(parent)

my_datetime.setDateTime(QDateTime.currentDateTime())

my_datetime.setCalendarPopup(True)

Methods:

currentDateTime()	returns the current date and time as a QDateTime object.
fromString(str, format)	creates a QDateTime object from a string formatted according to the specified format string.
toString(format)	returns the QDateTime object as a string formatted according to the specified format string.
date()	returns the date portion of the QDateTime object as a QDate object.
time()	returns the time portion of the QDateTime object as a QTime object.
addDays(int)	returns a QDateTime object that is int days later than the current QDateTime object.
addSecs(int)	returns a QDateTime object that is int seconds later than the current QDateTime object.

toMSecsSinceEpoch()	returns the number of milliseconds that have elapsed since January 1, 1970, 00:00:00.000 UTC.

Example:

```
from PyQt6.QtWidgets import QApplication, QWidget, QVBoxLayout,
QDateTimeEdit
from PyQt6.QtCore import QDateTime
import sys

app = QApplication(sys.argv)

window = QWidget()
window.setWindowTitle('QDateTimeEdit Example')
window.setGeometry(300, 300, 300, 200)

datetime_edit = QDateTimeEdit(window)
datetime_edit.setDateTime(QDateTime.currentDateTime())
datetime_edit.setCalendarPopup(True)

vbox = QVBoxLayout()
vbox.addWidget(datetime_edit)

window.setLayout(vbox)
window.show()

def datetime_changed(datetime):
    print('Selected datetime:', datetime.toString())

datetime_edit.dateTimeChanged.connect(datetime_changed)

sys.exit(app.exec())
```

In this example, we create a **QApplication** instance and a **QWidget** window. We then create a **QDateTimeEdit** widget and set its initial date and time to the current date and time using **QDateTime.currentDateTime()**. We also enable the calendar popup using **setCalendarPopup(True)**.

We create a **QVBoxLayout**, add the **QDateTimeEdit** to it, and set it as the layout of the window. Finally, we show the window.

We then define a slot function **datetime_changed** that takes the selected date and time as a **QDateTime** object. We connect the **dateTimeChanged** signal of the **QDateTimeEdit** to this slot function using the **connect** method.

When the user selects a new date and time in the **QDateTimeEdit**, it emits the **dateTimeChanged** signal, which is connected to the **datetime_changed** slot function. The **datetime_changed** function then prints a message to the console with the selected date and time in string format.

Output:

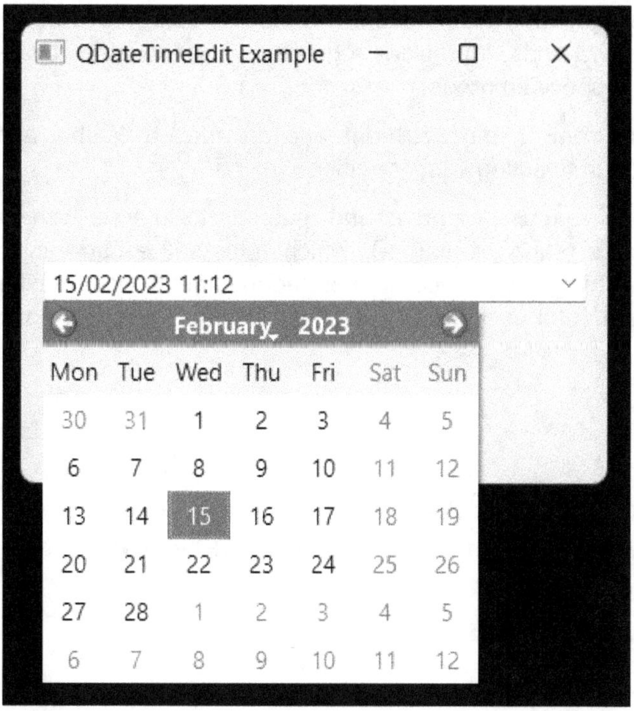

Very much like the QDateEdit example but with the addition of the time field. Just as you would expect.

QDial

QDial is a widget that allows users to select a value by dragging a dial or by clicking on its two ends. It provides a graphical user interface for selecting integer values within a specified range.

QDial inherits from **QAbstractSlider** and provides a flexible and customizable user interface for selecting integer values.

QDial provides various properties and methods to interact with its value, range, and appearance, such as **value()**, which returns the currently selected value, **setRange()**, which allows you to set the minimum and maximum selectable values, and **setNotchesVisible()**, which allows you to display notches around the dial.

Syntax:

Import the Widgets needed

from PyQt6.QtWidgets import QApplication, QDial, QWidget

Create the QDial

my_dial = QDial()

Customise the QDial properties if needed e.g.

my_dial.setMinimum(0)

my_dial.setMaximum(100)

my_dial.setSingleStep(1)

Here are some of the common methods used with **QDial:**

setValue(int value)	Sets the current value of the dial to the specified integer value.
value()	Returns the current value of the dial as an integer.
setMinimum(int minimum)	Sets the minimum value that the dial can represent.
minimum()	Returns the minimum value of the dial.
setMaximum(int maximum)	Sets the maximum value that the dial can represent.
maximum()	Returns the maximum value of the dial.

setNotchesVisible(bool visible)	Sets whether the notches on the dial should be visible or not.
setWrapping(bool enabled)	Sets whether the dial should wrap around from the maximum value to the minimum value.
setSingleStep(int step)	Sets the step size for the dial. The step size determines the amount by which the value changes when the dial is moved.
setTracking(bool enable)	Sets whether the dial emits signals while it is being dragged.

A very simple example with a dial that show a value on a label:

```
import sys
from PyQt6.QtWidgets import QApplication, QWidget, QDial, QVBoxLayout,
QLabel

app = QApplication(sys.argv)

# Create the dial
dial = QDial()
dial.setRange(0, 100)
dial.setNotchesVisible(True)
value = 0
dial.setValue(value)

# create the label
label=QLabel(str(value))

# Connect the valueChanged signal to a slot
def onValueChanged(value):
   label.setText(str(value))

# detect the QDial being turned
dial.valueChanged.connect(onValueChanged)

# Layout the dial
layout = QVBoxLayout()
layout.addWidget(dial)
layout.addWidget(label)
```

```
# Create the example widget
example = QWidget()
example.setLayout(layout)

# Show the example widget
example.show()

sys.exit(app.exec())
```

Output:

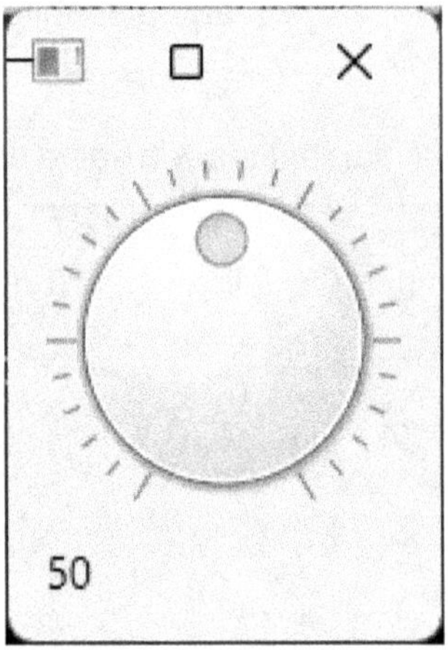

QDialog

QDialog is a widget that provides a dialog window for displaying messages, prompting the user for input, or performing other interactive tasks in a graphical user interface. This is typically used for things like the OK/Cancel popups (see example below).

Features of the QDialog widget include:

- It can be used as a top-level window or as a child window of another widget.
- It can be created as a modal or modeless dialog. Modal dialogs block input to other windows in the same application until they are closed, while modeless dialogs allow the user to interact with other windows while the dialog is open.
- It can be customised using many of the same properties and methods as other widgets, such as **setWindowTitle()** and **setLayout().**
- It provides several built-in buttons, such as Ok and Cancel, that can be used to close the dialog and return a result value to the calling function.

Syntax:

dialog = QDialog(parent=None, flags=Qt.WindowFlags())

Parent is the parent widget of the dialog, and flags is a combination of **Qt.WindowType** and **Qt.WindowFlag** that determine the dialog's behavior and appearance. The parent argument is optional and defaults to None, while the flags argument is also optional and defaults to **Qt.WindowFlags(),** which is an empty set of flags.

Methods:

setWindowTitle(title)	Sets the window title to title.
setWindowIcon(icon)	Sets the window icon to icon.
setFixedSize(width, height)	Sets the fixed size of the dialog to (width, height).
setModal(modal)	Sets the modality of the dialog. If modal is True, the dialog is modal and blocks user input to other windows in the same application. If modal is False, the dialog is non-modal and allows the user to interact with other parts of the application.
setLayout(layout)	Sets the layout manager of the dialog to layout.

exec()	Displays the dialog modally and blocks the program until the user closes it.
show()	Displays the dialog non-modally.
accept()	Closes the dialog and sets its result code to QDialog.Accepted.
reject()	Closes the dialog and sets its result code to QDialog.Rejected.
result()	Returns the result code of the dialog, which is either QDialog.Accepted or QDialog.Rejected.
close()	Closes the dialog.

Example:

```
from PyQt6.QtWidgets import QApplication, QDialog, QLabel,
QPushButton, QVBoxLayout, QHBoxLayout
import sys

app = QApplication(sys.argv)

# create the dialog
dialog = QDialog()
dialog.setWindowTitle('My Dialog')

# create the layout
layout = QVBoxLayout()

# add a label to the layout
label = QLabel('Do you want to save your changes?')
layout.addWidget(label)

# create a horizontal layout for the buttons
button_layout = QHBoxLayout()

# add an 'OK' button
ok_button = QPushButton('OK')
button_layout.addWidget(ok_button)

# add a 'Cancel' button
cancel_button = QPushButton('Cancel')
```

```
button_layout.addWidget(cancel_button)

# add the button layout to the main layout
layout.addLayout(button_layout)

# set the layout for the dialog
dialog.setLayout(layout)

# make the dialog modal
dialog.setModal(True)

# connect the buttons to slots
def on_ok_button_clicked():
    print('User clicked OK')
    dialog.accept()

def on_cancel_button_clicked():
    print('User clicked Cancel')
    dialog.reject()

ok_button.clicked.connect(on_ok_button_clicked)
cancel_button.clicked.connect(on_cancel_button_clicked)

# show the dialog
dialog.exec()
```

Output is Either:
User clicked OK
1

Or

User clicked Cancel

QDoubleSpinBox

QDoubleSpinBox allows the user to input and adjust numeric values with decimal precision. It is an extension of QSpinBox and provides additional functionality to handle floating-point numbers.

The **QDoubleSpinBox** widget provides a spin box with two arrow buttons for increasing or decreasing the value and an editable text field where the user can directly enter values. It supports a wide range of features, including:

> **Value Range:** You can set the minimum and maximum values that the spin box can represent using the **setMinimum** and **setMaximum** methods. The **minimum()** and **maximum()** methods allow you to retrieve the current minimum and maximum values.
>
> **Decimal Precision**: QDoubleSpinBox allows you to specify the number of decimal places using the **setDecimals** method. It affects the display of the value and the step size.
>
> **Step Size**: You can set the step size by calling **setSingleStep** to define the increment or decrement value when the user interacts with the arrow buttons or uses the keyboard. The **singleStep()** method retrieves the current step size.
>
> **Value Formatting**: **QDoubleSpinBox** provides various options for formatting the displayed value. You can set a prefix or suffix using **setPrefix** and **setSuffix** methods, respectively. Additionally, the **setSpecialValueText** method allows you to define a text representation for special values, such as "NaN" or "Infinity".
>
> **Signals and Slots: QDoubleSpinBox** emits signals such as **valueChanged** when the value changes, **editingFinished** when editing is complete, and more. These signals can be connected to custom slots to perform actions based on user input.

Syntax:

```
# Import the Widgets needed
from PyQt6.QtWidgets import QApplication, QDoubleSpinBox,
# Create the QDoubleSpinBox
spin_box = QDoubleSpinBox()
# Customise the QDoubleSpinBox properties if needed e.g.
spin_box.setMinimum(0.0)
spin_box.setMaximum(100.0)
spin_box.setDecimals(2)
spin_box.setSingleStep(0.1)
```

Some of the common methods used with QDoubleSpinBox:

setMinimum(double minimum)	Sets the minimum allowable value for the spin box.
minimum() -> double	Returns the current minimum value of the spin box.
setMaximum(double maximum)	Sets the maximum allowable value for the spin box.
maximum() -> double	Returns the current maximum value of the spin box.
setRange(double minimum, double maximum)	Sets both the minimum and maximum values simultaneously.
setValue(double value)	Sets the current value of the spin box.
value() -> double	Returns the current value of the spin box.
setDecimals(int decimals)	Sets the number of decimal places to display and accept.
decimals() -> int	Returns the current number of decimal places.
setSingleStep(double step)	Sets the increment or decrement step size for the spin box.
singleStep() -> double	Returns the current step size.
setPrefix(str prefix)	Sets the prefix to display before the value in the spin box.
prefix() -> str	Returns the current prefix.
setSuffix(str suffix)	Sets the suffix to display after the value in the spin box.
suffix() -> str	Returns the current suffix.
setSpecialValueText(str text)	Sets the text to display for special values like "NaN" or "Infinity".
specialValueText() -> str	Returns the current text for special values.

setReadOnly(bool enable)	Sets whether the spin box is read-only or editable.
isReadOnly() -> bool	Returns True if the spin box is read-only, False otherwise.

Example:

```
from PyQt6.QtWidgets import QApplication, QDoubleSpinBox,
QVBoxLayout, QWidget

app = QApplication([])

widget = QWidget()

layout = QVBoxLayout(widget)

spin_box = QDoubleSpinBox()
spin_box.setMinimum(0.0)
spin_box.setMaximum(100.0)
spin_box.setDecimals(2)
spin_box.setSingleStep(0.1)

layout.addWidget(spin_box)

widget.setLayout(layout)

widget.show()

app.exec()
```

Output:

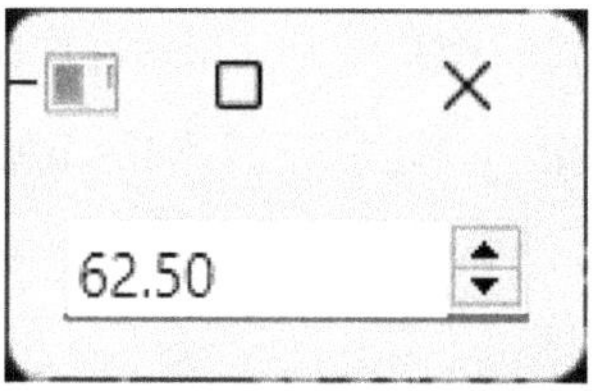

QFont

QFont is a class in that represents a font used for drawing text. It provides a way to specify various properties of a font, such as the family name, point size, weight, style, and so on. These properties can be set using the corresponding methods of the **QFont** class, and the current values of these properties can be retrieved using getter methods.

QFont is used in conjunction with various widgets in PyQt6 that display text, such as **QLabel**, **QTextEdit**, and **QPushButton**, among others. You can set the font of a widget using the **setFont** method of the widget, and the font will be used when drawing the text in the widget.

Syntax examples:

```
from PyQt6.QtGui import QFont
font = QFont()
font.setFamily("Arial")
font.setPointSize(18)
label.setFont(font)
```

or

```
from PyQt6.QtGui import QFont
font = QFont()
font = QFont("Arial", pointSize=36, italic=True)
label.setFont(font)
```

Here are some of the most commonly used methods of the **QFont** class:

setFamily(family: str):	Sets the font family name.
setPointSize(pointSize: int):	Sets the font point size.
setWeight(weight: int):	Sets the font weight.
setStyle(style: int):	Sets the font style.
setUnderline(underline: bool):	Sets whether the font should be underlined.
setStrikeOut(strikeOut: bool):	Sets whether the font should have a strikeout line.
setCapitalization(capitalization: int):	Sets the font capitalization.
setLetterSpacing(spacing: float):	Sets the font letter spacing.
setWordSpacing(spacing: float):	Sets the font word spacing.

setFixedPitch(fixedPitch: bool):	Sets whether the font is fixed-pitch.
setKerning(kerning: bool):	Sets whether kerning is used when drawing text with the font.

Example:

```
from PyQt6.QtGui import QFont
from PyQt6.QtWidgets import QApplication, QLabel, QWidget

app = QApplication([])
window = QWidget()
window.setWindowTitle('QFonts')
window.resize(250, 100)

# Create a label widget
label = QLabel("Font Test", window)

# Set the font properties for the label widget
font = QFont()
font.setFamily("Times New Roman")
font.setPointSize(36)
font.setItalic(True)
label.setFont(font)

window.show()
app.exec()
```

Output:

QFontComboxBox

QFontComboBox is a widget that displays a combobox (dropdown list) containing available font families. It allows users to select a font family from the list.

The QFontComboBox widget is derived from QComboBox and provides additional functionality specific to font selection. It automatically populates the combobox with the available font families installed on the system, allowing users to easily choose a font family.

Syntax:

Import the required modules

from PyQt6.QtWidgets import QApplication, QFontComboBox
create an instance of QFontComboBox:

font_combobox = QFontComboBox()

To retrieve the selected font family from the QFontComboBox, you can use the **currentFont()** method, which returns a QFont object:

selected_font = font_combobox.currentFont()

font_family = selected_font.family()

Here are some commonly used methods associated with **QFontComboBox**:

currentFont() -> QFont	Returns the currently selected font as a QFont object.
setCurrentFont(font: QFont)	Sets the currently selected font to the specified QFont.
setFontFilters(filters: QFontComboBox.FontFilters)	Sets the font filters to apply to the font list in the combobox. The filters parameter is a combination of QFontComboBox.FontFilters values that control which font families are displayed.
fontFilters() -> QFontComboBox.FontFilters	Returns the currently set font filters.
setWritingSystem(script: QFontDatabase.WritingSystem)	Sets the writing system for the font selection. The script parameter is a QFontDatabase.WritingSystem value that defines the writing system to filter fonts.

writingSystem() -> QFontDatabase.WritingSystem	Returns the currently set writing system for the font selection.
setMinimumPointSize(size: int)	Sets the minimum point size for fonts displayed in the combobox.
minimumPointSize() -> int	Returns the currently set minimum point size.
setMaximumPointSize(size: int)	Sets the maximum point size for fonts displayed in the combobox.
maximumPointSize() -> int	Returns the currently set maximum point size.
setFontFiltersEnabled(enabled: bool)	Enables or disables the font filters applied to the font list in the combobox.
isFontFiltersEnabled() -> bool	Returns True if font filters are enabled, False otherwise.

Note:

In **QFontDatabase.WritingSystem** is an enumeration that represents various writing systems or scripts used for different languages. It is used in conjunction with **QFontDatabase** to query and retrieve fonts based on specific writing systems.

The WritingSystem enumeration consists of the following values:

- **Any**: Represents any writing system.
- **Latin**: Represents the Latin writing system, which is used for many European languages.
- **Greek**: Represents the Greek writing system.
- **Cyrillic**: Represents the Cyrillic writing system, used for Slavic languages such as Russian and Bulgarian.
- **Armenian**: Represents the Armenian writing system.
- **Hebrew:** Represents the Hebrew writing system.
- **Arabic**: Represents the Arabic writing system such as Arabic and Persian.
- **Syriac:** Represents the Syriac writing system.
- **Thaana:** Represents the Thaana writing system for the Dhivehi language.
- **Devanagari**: Represents the Devanagari writing system, used for Hindi, Sanskrit, and other languages.
- **Bengali:** Represents the Bengali writing system.
- **Gurmukhi**: Represents the Gurmukhi writing system, used for Punjabi.

- **Gujarati:** Represents the Gujarati writing system.
- **Oriya:** Represents the Oriya writing system.
- **Tamil:** Represents the Tamil writing system.
- **Telugu**: Represents the Telugu writing system.
- **Kannada**: Represents the Kannada writing system.
- **Malayalam**: Represents the Malayalam writing system.
- **Sinhala:** Represents the Sinhala writing system.
- **Thai:** Represents the Thai writing system.
- **Lao:** Represents the Lao writing system.
- **Tibetan:** Represents the Tibetan writing system.
- **Myanmar:** Represents the Myanmar (Burmese) writing system.
- **Georgian**: Represents the Georgian writing system.
- **Khmer:** Represents the Khmer writing system for the Cambodian language.
- **SimplifiedChinese:** Represents the simplified Chinese writing system.
- **TraditionalChinese:** Represents the traditional Chinese writing system.
- **Japanese:** Represents the Japanese writing system.
- **Korean**: Represents the Korean writing system.
- **Vietnamese**: Represents the Vietnamese writing system.

These values can be used in **QFontDatabase** methods, such as **QFontDatabase.families()** or **QFontDatabase.fonts(),** to filter and retrieve fonts that support specific writing systems.

Example:

```
from PyQt6.QtWidgets import QApplication, QWidget, QVBoxLayout,
QFontComboBox, QLabel
from PyQt6.QtGui import QFont

# Create the application instance
app = QApplication([])

# Create a widget as the main window
window = QWidget()
window.setGeometry(100,100,300,150)
window.setWindowTitle("QFontComboBox Example")

# Create a label to show a font example
label = QLabel()
label.setText("This is the selected font family")
label.setFont(label_font)

# Create some initial font details for the label
label_font = QFont()
```

```
label_font.setFamily("Arial")
label_font.setPointSize(16)
label_font.setWeight(QFont.Bold)

layout = QVBoxLayout(window) # Create a layout for the main window

# Create a QFontComboBox instance and it's initial font
font_combo_box = QFontComboBox()
font_combo_box.setCurrentFont(label_font)

# Add the font combo box to the layout
layout.addWidget(font_combo_box)
layout.addWidget(label)

# Function to handle font selection changes
def on_font_changed(font):
    label.setFont(font)

# Connect the current font changed signal to the function
font_combo_box.currentFontChanged.connect(on_font_changed)

# Show the main window
window.show()

# Start the application event loop
app.exec()
```

Output:

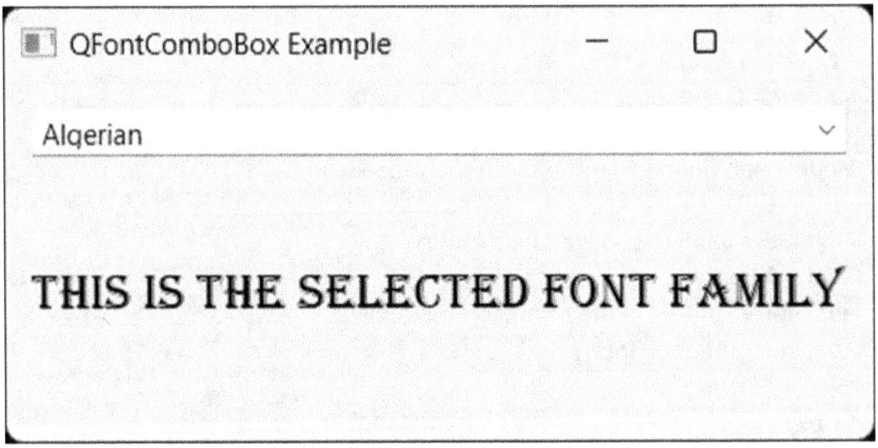

QFontDialog

QFontDialog is a dialog class that provides a standard font selection dialog for choosing fonts. It allows users to select a font family, style, size, and other font attributes.

Here are some key points about **QFontDialog**:

> **Font Selection:** QFontDialog displays a dialog window that presents a list of available fonts to choose from. It provides options to select the font family, style (e.g., bold, italic), size, and other font attributes.
>
> **Default Font:** You can set a default font using the **setFont()** method. The dialog will initially display this default font when opened
>
> **Current Font**: QFontDialog also provides a method called currentFont() to retrieve the font selected by the user in the dialog.
>
> **Font Dialog Options**: The dialog can be customised using various options. For example, you can enable or disable the font style selection, font size selection, and other options using the provided methods.
>
> **Executing the Dialog**: To open the **QFontDialog** and interact with it, you need to call the **exec()** method. It will block the program execution until the user closes the dialog.

Syntax:

Import the required modules:

from PyQt6.QtWidgets import QApplication, QWidget, QVBoxLayout, QPushButton, QFontDialog, QLabel

from PyQt6.QtGui import QFont

font, ok = QFontDialog.getFont(initial_font=None, parent=None, title='', options=QFontDialog.FontDialogOptions())

The **getFont()** function of **QFontDialog** is a static method that displays the font dialog and allows the user to select a font. It returns a tuple containing the selected font and a boolean value indicating whether the user accepted the selection (**ok**).

The parameters for the **getFont()** function are:

> **initial_font** (optional): Specifies the initial font to be shown in the font dialog. It is a QFont object that sets the initial font family, point size, and other properties. By default, it is set to None, which means no initial font is selected.
>
> **parent** (optional): Specifies the parent widget of the font dialog. It determines the dialog's ownership and its position relative to the parent widget. By default, it is set to None, indicating that the dialog has no parent.
>
> **title** (optional): Specifies the title of the font dialog window. By default, it is an empty string, resulting in a generic title.

options (optional): Specifies the font dialog options using QFontDialog.FontDialogOptions. It allows you to customise the behavior and appearance of the font dialog. By default, it uses the default options.

Methods (note **getFont()** described above):

staticFont() -> QFont	Returns the last font selected by the user in any font dialog. This method can be useful if you want to remember the last selected font and use it as the initial font the next time the font dialog is opened.
staticSetFont(font: QFont)	Sets the last font selected by the user in any font dialog. This method allows you to set the initial font for the next font dialog based on a previously selected font.
staticOptions() -> QFontDialog.FontDialogOptions	Returns the default font dialog options used by QFontDialog. This method returns the default font dialog options that determine the behavior and appearance of the font dialog.
staticSetOptions(options: QFontDialog.FontDialogOptions)	Sets the default font dialog options for QFontDialog. You can use this method to customise the default font dialog options used by QFontDialog.

Example:

```
from PyQt6.QtWidgets import QApplication, QWidget, QVBoxLayout,
QPushButton, QFontDialog, QLabel
from PyQt6.QtGui import QFont

# Create the application instance
app = QApplication([])

# Create a widget as the main window
window = QWidget()
window.setGeometry(100,100,300,150)
```

```
window.setWindowTitle("QFontDialog Example")

# Create a layout for the main window
layout = QVBoxLayout(window)

font = QFont()
font.setFamily("Arial")
font.setPointSize(16)
font.setWeight(QFont.Bold)

button = QPushButton("Press to select a font")

# Create a label to show a font example
label = QLabel()
label.setText("This is the selected font")
label.setFont(font)

# Add the font combo box to the layout
layout.addWidget(button)
layout.addWidget(label)

def show_font_dialog():
    font, ok = QFontDialog.getFont()
    if ok:
        label.setFont(font)
        label.setText(f"Selected Font: {font.family()}, Size: {font.pointSize()}")

button.clicked.connect(show_font_dialog)

# Show the main window
window.show()

# Start the application event loop
app.exec()
```

Output:

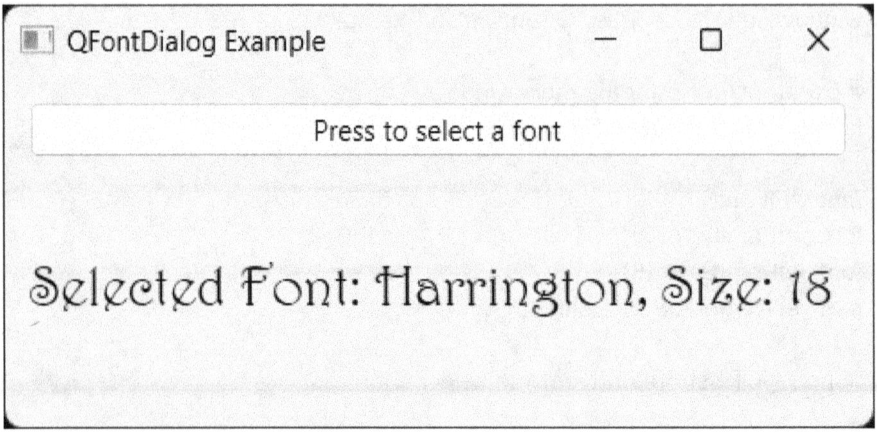

QGraphicsScene / QGraphicsView

QGraphicsScene is a class that provides a container for managing 2D graphical items. It represents a scene or canvas where you can add, remove, and manipulate graphics items such as shapes, images, and text. **QGraphicsView** is a widget that provides a framework for displaying and interacting with 2D graphical items in a customisable view. It is commonly used for creating interactive graphics applications, such as games, diagrams, and visualisations.

Key features and functionality include:

- **Scene-View Framework**: **QGraphicsView** follows the scene-view framework, where the graphical items are organized and managed in a **QGraphicsScene**, and the view widget (**QGraphicsView**) is responsible for displaying and interacting with the scene.
- **Graphics Scene**: The graphics scene (**QGraphicsScene**) serves as a container for managing the graphical items. It provides methods for adding, removing, and manipulating items, as well as handling events and collisions.
- **View Transformation**: **QGraphicsView** supports various transformation operations, including panning (scrolling), zooming, and rotating the view. These transformations can be applied programmatically or through user interactions.
- **Scene-View Coordination**: The scene and the view coordinate systems are separate but can be aligned and coordinated. **QGraphicsView** provides methods to map between the scene coordinates and the view coordinates, allowing you to convert positions and regions between the two systems.
- **Interaction and Events**: **QGraphicsView** handles user interactions, such as mouse and keyboard events, and provides signals for capturing and responding to these events. It supports selection of items, dragging and dropping, and other interaction mechanisms.

- **Performance Optimisation**: **QGraphicsView** employs various techniques to optimise rendering and performance, such as viewport updates, caching, and dynamic scene updates. It ensures efficient rendering of large scenes and responsiveness to user actions.

Graphics Items: QGraphicsScene is responsible for managing graphics items derived from the QGraphicsItem class. Graphics items can represent various visual elements, including shapes, images, text, and custom-drawn objects.

Coordinate System: QGraphicsScene has its own coordinate system, where the origin (0, 0) is located at the top-left corner of the scene. Positive x-coordinates extend towards the right, and positive y-coordinates extend downwards. You can work with scene coordinates when positioning and manipulating graphics items.

Item Management: QGraphicsScene provides methods to add, remove, and find graphics items within the scene. You can add items using addItem(), remove items using removeItem(), and retrieve items using items() or itemsBoundingRect().

Interaction and Event Handling: QGraphicsScene handles input events, such as mouse events and key events, to enable interaction with graphics items. You can override event handlers or use event filters to respond to user input within the scene.

Scene Rect: The scene has a bounding rectangle, known as the scene rect, that defines the extent of the scene. It can be automatically adjusted to encompass all the graphics items in the scene or manually set using setSceneRect().

Scene Background: You can set a background brush or background image for the scene using setBackgroundBrush() or setBackgroundBrush() respectively. This allows you to customise the visual appearance of the scene.

Item Grouping: QGraphicsScene supports grouping items together using QGraphicsItemGroup. Grouping allows you to treat multiple items as a single entity, making it easier to manipulate and manage them collectively.

Clipping and Viewport Management: The scene manages the clipping of graphics items to ensure that only visible portions are rendered. It also handles viewport management for QGraphicsView, providing automatic scrollbars when the scene size exceeds the viewport size.

Syntax:

Import the required modules e.g.:
from PyQt6.QtWidgets import QApplication, QGraphicsScene, QGraphicsView
from PyQt6.QtGui import QPixmap
Create a scene
scene = QGraphicsScene()
Create a view and set the scene
view = QGraphicsView(scene)

Commonly used methods of **QGraphicsScene**:

addItem(item)	Adds a **QGraphicsItem** or its derived class to the scene.
removeItem(item)	Removes a **QGraphicsItem** from the scene.
items()	Returns a list of all items in the scene.
clear()	Removes all items from the scene.
setSceneRect(rect)	Sets the bounding rectangle of the scene. It defines the extent of the scene and affects the view's scrollbars.
sceneRect()	Returns the current bounding rectangle of the scene.
itemAt(x, y)	Returns the topmost item at the specified coordinates.
itemsBoundingRect()	Returns the bounding rectangle that encloses all items in the scene.
collidingItems(item, mode)	Returns a list of items that collide with the given **item**.
setBackgroundBrush(brush)	Sets the brush used for the background of the scene.
setForegroundBrush(brush)	Sets the brush used for the foreground of the scene.
focusItem()	Returns the currently focused item in the scene.
setSelectionArea(area, mode)	Sets the selection area for the scene. The **area** parameter specifies the region of interest, and the **mode** parameter determines how the existing selection is updated.
views()	Returns a list of views currently displaying the scene.

update()	Forces an immediate redraw of the entire scene.

Commonly used methods of **QGraphicsView**:

setScene(scene)	Sets the graphics scene to be displayed in the view. The scene parameter should be an instance of **QGraphicsScene**.
scene()	Returns the currently set graphics scene.
setRenderHint(hint, enabled)	Enables or disables the specified rendering hint for the view. Rendering hints affect the way graphics items are rendered, providing options for performance optimization and visual quality.
setDragMode(mode)	Sets the drag mode for the view, determining how the user can interact with the scene by dragging items. The available **mode** options include **NoDrag**, **ScrollHandDrag**, **RubberBandDrag**, and **CustomDrag**.
resetMatrix()	Resets the view's transformation matrix to its identity state, effectively removing any scaling, rotation, or translation applied to the view.
setViewportUpdateMode (mode)	Sets the mode for updating the viewport when the scene changes. The available **mode** options include **FullViewportUpdate**, **MinimalViewportUpdate**, **SmartViewportUpdate**, and **BoundingRectViewportUpdate**.

setRenderHint(hint, enabled)	Enables or disables the specified rendering hint for the view. Rendering hints affect the way graphics items are rendered, providing options for performance optimization and visual quality.
centerOn(item)	Centers the view on the specified **item**, ensuring that the item is visible in the view.
setInteractive(enabled)	Enables or disables the interactive mode of the view. When disabled, user interactions such as mouse events and keyboard events are ignored.
setTransformationAnchor(anchor)	Sets the anchor point for the view's transformations. The **anchor** parameter specifies whether the transformations should be applied relative to the view's center, the mouse position, or the anchor point specified by **setTransformOriginPoint()**.

Example:

```
from PyQt6.QtWidgets import QApplication, QGraphicsScene,
QGraphicsView
from PyQt6.QtGui import QPixmap

app = QApplication([])

# Create a scene
scene = QGraphicsScene()

# Load the image
pixmap = QPixmap("car.png")

# Create a pixmap item
pixmap_item = scene.addPixmap(pixmap)

# Create a view and set the scene
view = QGraphicsView(scene)

# Show the view
view.show()

app.exec()
```

Output:

QIcon

QIcon is a class that represents an icon, which is typically used to represent graphical elements such as application icons, toolbar icons, or menu icons. QIcon provides methods to load and manipulate icons, allowing you to set them on various PyQt6 widgets.

There are a number of ways in which you can use QIcon to load an image to use as an Icon. These include:

- Load an icon from an image file
- Load an icon from the system's icon theme
- Load an icon from a Qt resource file
- Load from QPixmap

Example:

```
from PyQt6.QtGui import QIcon

icon = QIcon("path/to/icon.png") # Load an icon from an image file

# Using built-in icons
icon = QIcon.fromTheme("edit-cut") # Load an icon from the system's icon
theme
icon = QIcon(":/icons/my_icon.png") # Load an icon from a Qt resource file

from PyQt6.QtGui import QPixmap

pixmap = QPixmap("path/to/image.png")
icon = QIcon.fromPixmap(pixmap)
```

Syntax:
Import the modules required

from PyQt6.QtWidgets import QPushButton

from PyQt6.QtGui import QIcon

button = QPushButton()

button.setIcon(icon)

Here are some commonly used methods associated with **QIcon**:

fromTheme(name: str) -> QIcon	Creates an QIcon object from a named icon theme. The name parameter specifies the name of the icon in the theme.
fromTheme(name: str, fallback: QIcon) -> QIcon	Creates an QIcon object from a named icon theme, using the fallback QIcon if the named icon is not found.
fromTheme(name: str, fallback: Union[QIcon, None] = None) -> QIcon	Creates an QIcon object from a named icon theme, using the fallback QIcon if provided, or a default fallback if not provided.
fromPixmap(pixmap: QPixmap) -> QIcon	Creates an QIcon object from a QPixmap. The pixmap is used as the icon representation.
availableSizes(mode: Qt.IconMode = Qt.IconMode.Normal, state: Qt.IconState = Qt.IconState.On) -> List[QSize]	Returns a list of available sizes for the icon, optionally filtered by the specified mode and state.
actualSize(size: QSize, mode: Qt.IconMode = Qt.IconMode.Normal, state: Qt.IconState = Qt.IconState.On) -> QSize	Returns the actual size of the icon that best fits the specified size, based on the available sizes and the specified mode and state.
pixmap(size: QSize, mode: Qt.IconMode = Qt.IconMode.Normal, state: Qt.IconState = Qt.IconState.On) -> QPixmap	Returns a QPixmap representation of the icon with the specified size, mode, and state.

pixmap(width: int, height: int, mode: Qt.IconMode = Qt.IconMode.Normal, state: Qt.IconState = Qt.IconState.On) -> QPixmap	Returns a QPixmap representation of the icon with the specified width, height, mode, and state.
name() -> str	Returns the name of the icon.
isNull() -> bool	Returns True if the QIcon is null, i.e., it does not contain any icon data.
isMask() -> bool	Returns True if the QIcon represents a mask, i.e., it is used for masking other icons.

Example:

```
from PyQt6.QtWidgets import QApplication, QLabel, QVBoxLayout,
QWidget
from PyQt6.QtGui import QIcon
import sys

app = QApplication(sys.argv)

window = QWidget()
layout = QVBoxLayout(window)

label = QLabel()
icon = QIcon("car.png")
label.setPixmap(icon.pixmap(64, 64))  # Set the pixmap representation of
the icon on the label

layout.addWidget(label)
window.show()

sys.exit(app.exec())
```

Here is the output. Please note that the **car.png** file used is the same one as used in the **QPixmap** example later – see that section to see the file displayed by **QPixmap**..

The file **car.png** (reduced to fit on the page)

QImage

QImage is a class that provides a platform-independent representation of an image. It can be used for loading, manipulating, and saving images. Here are some key points about **QImage**:

QImage can handle various image formats, including different colour depths and channel orders. It supports formats like RGB, ARGB, grayscale, and indexed colour.

- **QImage** can be constructed from different sources such as file paths, raw data, or existing **QPixmaps**.
- **QImage** provides methods for accessing and modifying individual pixels of the image.
- **QImage** can be used for performing image transformations like scaling, rotating, and mirroring.
- **QImage** supports operations like cropping, copying, and composition with other images.
- **QImage** can be saved to disk in various image formats, such as PNG, JPEG, BMP, and GIF.
- **QImage** provides information about its size, depth, format, and other properties.
- **QImage** can be used in combination with QPainter to perform painting operations on the image.
- **QImage** can be converted to and from other image formats like QPixmap and PIL (Python Imaging Library) images.

Syntax:

Import the required modules

from PyQt6.QtGui import QImage

Create an image (note the Syntax differs from PyQt5) so image = QImage(width, height, format) e.g:

image = QImage(200, 100, QImage.Format.Format_RGB32)

Some commonly used image formats include:

- **QImage.Format.Format_Mono**: 1-bit per pixel, black and white image.
- **QImage.Format.Format.MonoLSB**: 1-bit per pixel, black and white image with the least significant bit (LSB) first.
- **QImage.Format.Format_Indexed8**: 8-bit per pixel, indexed color image.
- **QImage.Format.Format_RGB32**: 32-bit per pixel, RGB image without alpha channel.
- **QImage.Format.Format_ARGB32**: 32-bit per pixel, ARGB image with alpha channel.
- **QImage.Format.Format_ARGB32_Premultiplied:** 32-bit per pixel, ARGB image with premultiplied alpha channel.

These are just a few examples of the image formats available in QImage. There are additional formats, such as **RGB16**, **RGB555**, and **RGB888**, as well as various image formats for specific platforms and use cases.

Here are some commonly used methods:

pixel(x: int, y: int) -> int	Returns the pixel value at the specified coordinates (x, y) as an integer.
setPixel(x: int, y: int, color: int) -> None	Sets the pixel value at the specified coordinates (x, y) to the given colour, which should be an integer representing the pixel colour.
pixelColor(x: int, y: int) -> QColor	Returns the QColor object representing the pixel colour at the specified coordinates (x, y).
setPixelColor(x: int, y: int, color: QColor) -> None	Sets the pixel colour at the specified coordinates (x, y) using the provided QColor object.
fill(color: Union[Qt.GlobalColor, QColor]) -> None	Fills the entire image with the specified colour.
load(fileName: str, format: Optional[str] = None) -> bool	Loads the image from the specified file. Optionally, you can specify the file format.
save(fileName: str, format: Optional[str] = None, quality: int = -1) -> bool	Saves the image to the specified file. Optionally, you can specify the file format and image quality.

scaled(width: int, height: int, aspectRatioMode: Qt.AspectRatioMode = Qt.AspectRatioMode.IgnoreAspectRatio, transformMode: Qt.TransformationMode = Qt.TransformationMode.SmoothTransformation) -> QImage	Returns a scaled copy of the image with the specified width and height. You can specify the aspect ratio mode and transformation mode.
copy() -> QImage	Returns a deep copy of the image.
isNull() -> bool	Checks if the image is null or empty.
size() -> QSize	Returns the size (width and height) of the image as a QSize object.
width() -> int	Returns the width of the image in pixels.
height() -> int	Returns the height of the image in pixels.
format() -> int	Returns the format of the image as an integer.
depth() -> int	Returns the number of bits used to represent each pixel.
convertToFormat(format: int, conversionFlags: Union[Qt.ImageConversionFlags, Qt.ImageConversionFlag] = Qt.ImageConversionFlag.AutoColor) -> QImage	Converts the image to the specified format.

Example:

```
from PyQt6.QtCore import Qt
from PyQt6.QtGui import QGuiApplication, QImage, QPainter, QColor,
QPixmap, QFont

app = QGuiApplication([])

# Create a QImage with a size of 200x200 pixels and RGB32 format
```

```
image = QImage(200, 200, QImage.Format.Format_RGB32)

# Create a QPainter object to perform painting operations on the image
painter = QPainter(image)

# Set the background color of the image to white
painter.fillRect(image.rect(), Qt.GlobalColor.white)

# Draw a red rectangle on the image
painter.setPen(Qt.GlobalColor.red)
painter.drawRect(50, 50, 100, 100)

# Draw a green ellipse on the image
painter.setPen(Qt.GlobalColor.green)
painter.setBrush(Qt.GlobalColor.green)
painter.drawEllipse(75, 75, 50, 50)

# Draw text on the image
painter.setPen(Qt.GlobalColor.black)
painter.setFont(QFont("Arial", 12))
painter.drawText(20, 180, "Hello, PyQt6 user!")

# End the painting operations
painter.end()

# Save the image to a file
image.save("newimage.png")

# Display image properties
width = image.width()
height = image.height()
format = image.format()
depth = image.depth()

# Convert QImage to QPixmap for display purposes
pixmap = QPixmap.fromImage(image)
```

Output – this is the file **newimage,png.** For information, the Square is red and the circle is green.

Hello, PyQt6 user!

In this example, we have use **QGuiApplication** rather than **QApplication.** Counter-intuitively, you can use **QGuiApplication** when you are developing a non-GUI application or an application that does not require a windowing system, such as a command-line tool or a background service. **QGuiApplication** provides the necessary event loop and platform integration for such applications. It focuses on handling input events, managing resources, and interacting with the underlying system.

QInputDialog

The **QInputDialog** class provides a simple way to create dialog boxes that prompt the user for input. It is a pre-built dialog that allows you to obtain different types of input from the user, such as text, numbers, or items from a list.

Here are some key points about **QInputDialog**:

Input Types: QInputDialog supports various types of input, including text, integers, floating-point numbers, and selection from a list.

Dialog Types: QInputDialog provides different dialog types based on the input you want to obtain:

getText(): Prompt the user to enter a single line of text.

getInt(): Prompt the user to enter an integer value.

getDouble(): Prompt the user to enter a floating-point number.

getItem(): Prompt the user to select an item from a list.

Default Values: You can set default values for the input fields to provide initial suggestions or values to the user.

Validation and Constraints: QInputDialog allows you to specify validators and constraints on the input, ensuring that the user enters valid values within the specified range or format.

Return Values: Depending on the dialog type, QInputDialog returns the input value(s) entered by the user.

Syntax:

Import the required modules:

from PyQt6.QtWidgets import QApplication, QInputDialog

to get text

text, ok = QInputDialog.getText(parent, title, label, options)

where:

- **parent**: The parent widget of the dialog (can be None).
- **title:** The title or caption of the dialog.
- **label:** The label or prompt text displayed to the user.
- **options:** Additional options or flags (if any).

Other methods:

Get Integer

value, ok = QInputDialog.getInt(parent, title, label, value, min, max, step, options)

- **parent:** The parent widget of the dialog (can be None).
- **title**: The title or caption of the dialog.
- **label:** The label or prompt text displayed to the user.
- **value**: The default value for the input field.
- **min:** The minimum allowed value.
- **max:** The maximum allowed value.
- **step:** The step size or increment for the input field.
- **options:** Additional options or flags (optional).

Get Item (from a list):

item, ok = QInputDialog.getItem(parent, title, label, items, current, editable, options)

- **parent:** The parent widget of the dialog (can be None).
- **title:** The title or caption of the dialog.
- **label:** The label or prompt text displayed to the user.
- **items:** The list of items to display for selection.
- **current:** The initially selected item.
- **editable**: Flag indicating if the user can enter a custom item.
- **options:** Additional options or flags (optional).

In all cases, the method returns two values: the input value entered by the user (text, value, item) and a boolean indicating whether the user clicked OK (ok) or Cancel. You can adjust the arguments and customise the dialog based on your specific requirements.

In addition to these methods, **QInputDialog** also provides other utility methods:

getIntRange() - Get the default minimum and maximum values for integer input:

min, max, step = QInputDialog.getIntRange()

doubleDecimals() - Get the default number of decimal places for floating-point input:

decimals = QInputDialog.doubleDecimals()

Example:

```
from PyQt6.QtWidgets import QApplication, QInputDialog

# Create a QApplication instance
app = QApplication([])

# Prompt the user to enter a text
text, ok = QInputDialog.getText(None, "Text Input", "Enter your name:")

# Check if the user clicked OK and entered a value
if ok:
    print("Entered Text:", text)
else:
    print("No text entered.")

# Close the application
app.quit()
```

Output:

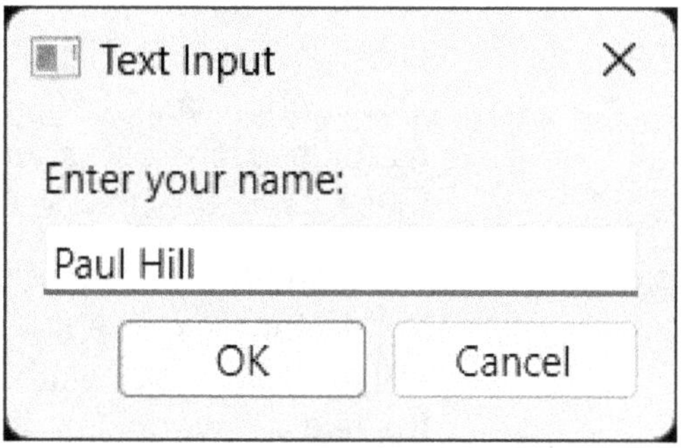

And also output to the console:

Entered Text: Paul Hill

QLabel

QLabel is a widget that can display text or an image.

Syntax:

my_label = QLabel(text, parent)

An example of configuring a label could be:

```
label = QLabel(window)
label.setText("Label Text goes here")
label.setFont(QFont("Arial", 20, QFont.Bold))
```

Some common methods of the **QLabel** widget in PyQt:

setText(text)	Sets the text displayed by the label to the given text.
setPixmap(pixmap)	Sets the image displayed by the label to the given pixmap.
setAlignment(alignment)	Sets the alignment of the text or pixmap within the label. The alignment parameter can be one of Qt.AlignLeft, Qt.AlignRight, Qt.AlignTop, Qt.AlignBottom, Qt.AlignCenter, Qt.AlignJustify, or a combination of these using the bitwise OR operator (|).
setWordWrap(on)	Sets whether the label should wrap its text to the next line if it's too long to fit within the label's width. If on is True, the text will wrap; if on is False, the text will be truncated if it's too long.
setStyleSheet(styleSheet)	Sets the style sheet used to style the label. The styleSheet parameter is a string containing CSS-like style rules.
clear()	Clears the text and image displayed by the label.
sizeHint()	Returns the recommended size of the label based on its contents.
setToolTip(text)	Sets the tool tip text displayed when the mouse pointer hovers over the label.

setIndent(num)	Sets the indent of the label's text, measured in pixels.
setMargin(num)	Sets the margin around the label's contents, measured in pixels.
setScaledContents(on)	Sets whether the label's pixmap should be scaled to fit within the label's size. If on is True, the pixmap will be scaled; if on is False, the pixmap will be displayed at its actual size.

QLCDNumber

QLCDNumber is a widget provided by PyQt6 that displays a numeric value in a digital format similar to an LCD (Liquid Crystal Display) screen. It is commonly used to show numerical values or measurements in applications that require a visual representation of numeric data.

The QLCDNumber widget supports various features, including:

- Displaying integer or floating-point values with a specified number of digits.
- Customizable appearance, such as segment style, colour, and background.
- Support for negative values.
- Formatting options, including decimal point position and leading zeros.
- Animation effects for value changes.

Syntax:

Import the required modules

from PyQt6.QtWidgets import QApplication, QLCDNumber, QVBoxLayout, QWidget

Create an instance of QLCDNumber:

lcd_number = QLCDNumber()

You can set the displayed value using the **display()** method:

lcd_number.display(integer or float)

Methods:

display(value: Union[int, float])	Sets the displayed value to the specified integer or floating-point value.
value() -> float	Returns the currently displayed numeric value as a float.
setDigitCount(count: int)	Sets the number of digits to display. The count parameter specifies the desired number of digits.
setSmallDecimalPoint(enabled: bool)	Controls whether the decimal point is displayed as small or large.

setMode(mode: QLCDNumber.Mode)	Sets the display mode for the numeric value. The mode parameter is a QLCDNumber.Mode value that determines how the number is displayed (e.g., decimal, hexadecimal, octal).
setSegmentStyle(style: QLCDNumber.SegmentStyle)	Sets the segment style for the display. The style parameter is a QLCDNumber.SegmentStyle value that specifies the appearance of the segments (e.g., flat, raised).
setStyleSheet(styleSheet: str)	Sets the style sheet for customizing the appearance of the QLCDNumber widget using CSS-like syntax.
setPalette(palette: QPalette)	Sets the palette for customizing the colour scheme of the widget.
setAutoFillBackground(enabled: bool)	Controls whether the widget automatically fills its background with the current palette colour.
setFrameStyle(style: int)	Sets the frame style for the widget.
setNumDigits(digits: int)	Sets the number of digits to display, which is equivalent to setDigitCount().
setSmallDecimalPoint(enabled: bool)	Controls whether the decimal point is displayed as small or large.

Example:

```
from PyQt6.QtWidgets import QApplication, QLCDNumber, QPushButton,
QVBoxLayout, QWidget
import sys

def increase_value():
    current_value = lcd_number.value()
    lcd_number.display(current_value + 1)

def decrease_value():
    current_value = lcd_number.value()
    lcd_number.display(current_value - 1)

# Create the application
app = QApplication(sys.argv)

# Create the main window
window = QWidget()
window.setWindowTitle("QLCDNumber Example")
# set window position x, y, width, height
window.setGeometry(100, 100, 250, 250)

# Create a vertical layout for the window
layout = QVBoxLayout(window)

# Create a QLCDNumber widget
lcd_number = QLCDNumber()
lcd_number.setDigitCount(3)  # Display three digits

# Create a QPushButton to increase the value
button1 = QPushButton("Increase")
button1.clicked.connect(increase_value)
# Create a QPushButton to increase the value
button2 = QPushButton("Decrease")
button2.clicked.connect(decrease_value)

# Add the widgets to the layout
layout.addWidget(lcd_number)
layout.addWidget(button1)
layout.addWidget(button2)

# Show the window
```

```
window.show()

# Start the event loop
sys.exit(app.exec())
```
Output:

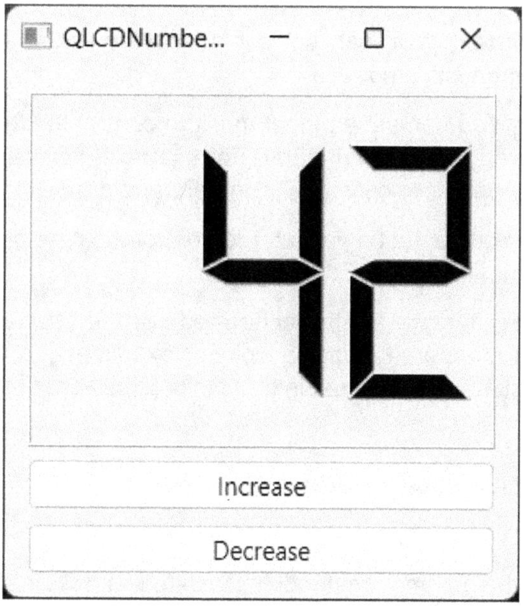

QLineEdit

A single-line text input box for user input.

QLineEdit is a useful widget that allows you to create text input fields. It has a lot of options and features to customise its behavior and appearance. Some of the common features of **QLineEdit** are:

Placeholder text: You can set a placeholder text to be displayed in the QLineEdit when it is empty.

Input Mask: You can set an input mask to control the format of the text that can be entered into the QLineEdit. For example, you can set an input mask for a phone number to only allow numbers and dashes to be entered.

Validation: You can set a validator to control the type of characters that can be entered into the **QLineEdit**.

Echo mode: You can set the echo mode of the **QLineEdit** to control how the text that is entered is displayed. For example, you can set it to display asterisks instead of the actual text to mask passwords.

Syntax:

my_entry_text = QLineEdit(parent)

Here are some of the common methods associated with **QLineEdit**:

setText(text)	Sets the text displayed in the QLineEdit to the specified text value.
text()	Returns the current text displayed in the QLineEdit.
setPlaceholderText(text)	Sets the placeholder text to be displayed when the QLineEdit is empty.
setReadOnly(bool)	Sets whether the QLineEdit is read only or not.
setValidator(validator)	Sets the validator for the QLineEdit to control the type of characters that can be entered.
setInputMask(mask)	Sets the input mask for the QLineEdit to control the format of the text that can be entered.
setEchoMode(mode)	Sets the echo mode of the QLineEdit to control how the text that is entered is displayed.

setMaxLength(length)	Sets the maximum length of the text that can be entered into the QLineEdit.
selectAll()	Selects all the text in the QLineEdit.
deselect()	Deselects the current text in the QLineEdit.
cursorPosition()	Returns the current cursor position in the QLineEdit.
setCursorPosition(pos)	Sets the cursor position to the specified pos value

Example:

```
from PyQt6.QtWidgets import QApplication, QLineEdit, QWidget,
QVBoxLayout, QLabel
from PyQt6.QtGui import QFont

app = QApplication([])
window = QWidget()

layout = QVBoxLayout()

line_edit = QLineEdit()
line_edit.setPlaceholderText("Enter your name")

label = QLabel("Placeholder")
label.setFont(QFont("Helvetica", 18))

layout.addWidget(line_edit)
layout.addWidget(label)

# Connect the textChanged signal of QLineEdit to the update_name slot
def update_name(text):
   # Update the text of the QLabel with the current text of the QLineEdit
   label.setText("Hello " + text)

# the next line detects the change in text entered
line_edit.textChanged.connect(update_name)

window.setLayout(layout)
window.show()
app.exec()
```

Output:

QMenu and QMenuBar

QMenu and **QMenuBar** are two classes in **PyQt6** that provide a way to create and manage menus and menu bars in a graphical user interface.

QMenu is a class that represents a popup menu that can be displayed anywhere in a GUI application. It can contain a list of menu items, each of which can perform a specific action or trigger a particular event. A **QMenu** can be created and added to a parent widget, such as a **QMainWindow**, by calling the **addMenu()** method of the parent widget. Menu items can then be added to the **QMenu** using the **addAction()** method.

QAction

QAction is a class in the **PyQt6** toolkit that represents an action that can be triggered by a user in a graphical user interface (GUI) application. It can be used to add menu items, toolbar buttons, or keyboard shortcuts to a GUI application. Import it using **from PyQt6.QtGui import QAction**

A **QAction** object has a variety of properties that can be customised, such as its text, icon, tooltip, and keyboard shortcut. When the user triggers the **QAction**, it emits a triggered signal, which can be connected to a slot function to perform a specific action, such as opening a file or saving changes.

QAction can be used to create menu items by adding them to a **QMenu** object using the **addAction()** method. It can also be used to create toolbar buttons by adding them to a **QToolBar** object using the **addAction()** method. Keyboard shortcuts can be added to **QAction** objects using the **setShortcut()** method.

QMenuBar

QMenuBar is a class that represents a menu bar that is typically displayed at the top of a main window in a GUI application. It can contain a list of menu items, each of which can either display a **QMenu** or perform a specific action. A **QMenuBar** can be created and added to a parent widget, such as a **QMainWindow**, by calling the **setMenuBar()** method of the parent widget. Menu items can then be added to the **QMenuBar** using the **addMenu()** method.

Example:

```
import sys
from PyQt6.QtWidgets import QApplication, QMainWindow, QMenu
from PyQt6.QtGui import QAction

app = QApplication(sys.argv)

window = QMainWindow() # Create the main window
window.setWindowTitle("Menu Example")

# Create a menu bar and add it to the main window
menubar = window.menuBar()

# Create a File menu and add it to the menu bar
file_menu = QMenu("File", window)
menubar.addMenu(file_menu)

# Create a Quit action and add it to the File menu
quit_action = QAction("Quit", window)
quit_action.triggered.connect(app.quit)
file_menu.addAction(quit_action)

window.show() # Show the main window

sys.exit(app.exec())
```

QMessageBox

This dialog class is used to display a message to the user, such as an error message or a confirmation message. It has different types of buttons that can be added to it, such as "Ok", "Yes", "No", and "Cancel".

QMessageBox is a class that provides a simple way to display dialog boxes for displaying messages, asking for user confirmation, or requesting input from the user. It is typically used to show standard modal message boxes in a graphical user interface (GUI) application.

QMessageBox supports different types of message boxes, including information, warning, critical, question, and custom boxes. Here are some key features and methods of QMessageBox:

Predefined Types: QMessageBox provides predefined types for common message box scenarios:

Information: Displays an information icon and provides information to the user.

Warning: Displays a warning icon and alerts the user about a non-critical issue.

Critical: Displays a critical icon and indicates a critical error or problem.

Question: Displays a question icon and asks the user for confirmation or a choice.

Buttons and Default Button: You can specify the buttons to be shown in the message box, such as OK, Yes, No, Cancel, etc. The **QMessageBox** class provides predefined button options, and you can also customise the button text and order. You can set a default button that is triggered when the user presses Enter.

Icon: QMessageBox supports different icons to visually represent the type of message. Icons include information, warning, critical error, question, and no icon.

Standard Button Return Values: QMessageBox provides standard button return values to determine which button the user clicked. These values include:

QMessageBox.StandardButton.Yes
QMessageBox.StandardButton.No
QMessageBox.StandardButton.Ok
QMessageBox.StandardButton.Cancel

Static Methods: QMessageBox offers static methods for convenience, allowing you to quickly create and display message boxes without instantiating the class explicitly. Examples of static methods include:

QMessageBox.information()
QMessageBox.warning()

QMessageBox.critical()

QMessageBox.question()

Additional Customisation: QMessageBox allows further customisation, such as setting a custom title, message text, detailed text, and adding additional widgets to the message box, such as checkboxes, text input fields, or progress bars.

Syntax:

Import the required modules:

from PyQt6.QtWidgets import QMessageBox

Create the message box

message_box = QMessageBox()

set the required options e.g.

message_box.setText("warning message.")

Here are some commonly used methods:

setIcon(icon)	Sets the icon for the message box. The icon parameter can be one of the QMessageBox.Icon values, such as QMessageBox.Icon.Information, QMessageBox.Icon.Warning, QMessageBox.Icon.Critical, or QMessageBox.Icon.Question.
setText(text)	Sets the main text message displayed in the message box.
setInformativeText(text)	Sets additional informative text that provides more details or explanations.
setWindowTitle(title)	Sets the title of the message box window.

setStandardButtons(buttons)	Sets the standard buttons to be displayed in the message box. The buttons parameter can be a combination of QMessageBox.StandardButton values, such as QMessageBox.StandardButton.Ok, QMessageBox.StandardButton.Cancel, QMessageBox.StandardButton.Yes, QMessageBox.StandardButton.No, etc.
setDefaultButton(button)	Sets the default button that is triggered when the user presses Enter. The button parameter should be one of the standard buttons specified in setStandardButtons().
exec()	Displays the message box as a modal dialog and waits for the user to close it. The method returns the result (a QMessageBox.StandardButton value) indicating which button the user clicked.

there are other methods available to further customise the message box, such as:

- **setDetailedText(text):** Sets a detailed text that provides more extensive information.
- **setCheckBox(checkbox):** Adds a checkbox to the message box.
- **addButton(button):** Adds a custom button to the message box.
- **setDefaultButton(button):** Sets a custom button as the default button.
- **buttonRole(button):** Retrieves the role of a specific button.
- **buttonText(button):** Retrieves the text of a specific button.
- **buttonClicked.connect(slot):** Connects a slot to the signal emitted when a button is clicked.

Example:

```
from PyQt6.QtWidgets import QMessageBox, QApplication

app = QApplication([])

message_box = QMessageBox()
message_box.setIcon(QMessageBox.Icon.Information)
message_box.setText("This is an information message.")
message_box.setWindowTitle("Information")
message_box.setStandardButtons(QMessageBox.StandardButton.Ok)

result = message_box.exec()

if result == QMessageBox.StandardButton.Ok:
    print("OK button clicked")

app.exec()
```

Output:

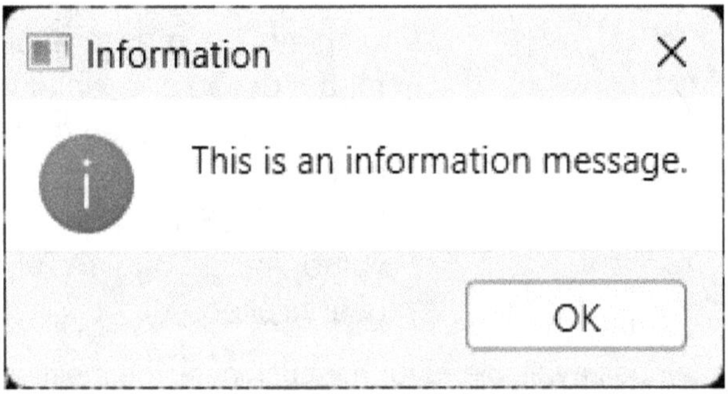

QPainter

QPainter is a class in the Qt framework that provides a high-level API for rendering 2D graphics on widgets and other paint devices. It is commonly used for drawing shapes, text, and images on the screen.

The **QPainter** class uses a painter metaphor to describe the painting process. To use **QPainter,** you create an instance of the class and pass it a paint device to draw on, such as a **QWidget** or **QPixmap**. You then use **QPainter's** functions to draw on the device, and the changes are automatically displayed on the screen.

Some of the functions provided by **QPainter** include drawing lines, rectangles, ellipses, and polygons. You can also draw text with different fonts, colours, and alignments, and load and draw images in various formats.

Syntax:

First import the modules that you will require e.g.

from PyQt6.QtWidgets import QApplication, QWidget

from PyQt6.QtGui import QPainter, QColor

create a painter object:

painter = QPainter()

you can paint on a QPixmap, a QImage or a QWidget

painter.begin(widget) # widget can be any paint device, such as a QPixmap, QImage, or QWidget

Example painting methods:

painter.drawLine(x1, y1, x2, y2)

painter.drawRect(x, y, width, height)

painter.drawText(x, y, text)

When finished, you can end the painting

painter.end()

Here are some commonly used methods associated with **QPainter**:

begin(device: Union[QPaintDevice, QPaintDevice.Window, QPaintDevice.Pixmap])	Begins painting on the specified device.
end()	Ends the painting operation.
setPen(pen: QPen)	Sets the pen used for drawing lines and outlines.

setBrush(brush: QBrush)	Sets the brush used for filling shapes.
setFont(font: QFont)	Sets the font used for drawing text.
setRenderHint(hint: QPainter.RenderHint, on: bool = True)	Enables or disables the specified rendering hint.
drawPoint(x: int, y: int)	Draws a single point at the specified coordinates.
drawLine(x1: int, y1: int, x2: int, y2: int)	Draws a line between the specified points.
drawRect(x: int, y: int, width: int, height: int)	Draws a rectangle with the specified coordinates, width, and height.
drawEllipse(x: int, y: int, width: int, height: int)	Draws an ellipse inscribed within the specified rectangle.
drawText(x: int, y: int, text: str)	Draws the specified text at the specified coordinates.
drawPixmap(target: QRect, pixmap: QPixmap, source: QRect = QRect())	Draws a pixmap onto the target rectangle.
save()	Saves the current state of the painter (pen, brush, font, etc.).
restore()	Restores the previously saved state of the painter.

Example:

```
from PyQt6.QtWidgets import QApplication, QWidget
from PyQt6.QtGui import QPainter, QColor
import sys

def paintEvent(event):
    painter = QPainter()
    painter.begin(widget)
    painter.setPen(QColor("red"))
    painter.drawLine(50, 50, 200, 200)
    painter.setBrush(QColor("blue"))
    painter.drawRect(100, 100, 150, 150)
    painter.setPen(QColor("green"))
```

```
    painter.drawText(50, 50, "Hello, World!")
    painter.end()

app = QApplication(sys.argv)

widget = QWidget()
widget.resize(300, 300)
widget.show()

widget.paintEvent = paintEvent

sys.exit(app.exec())
```

Output:

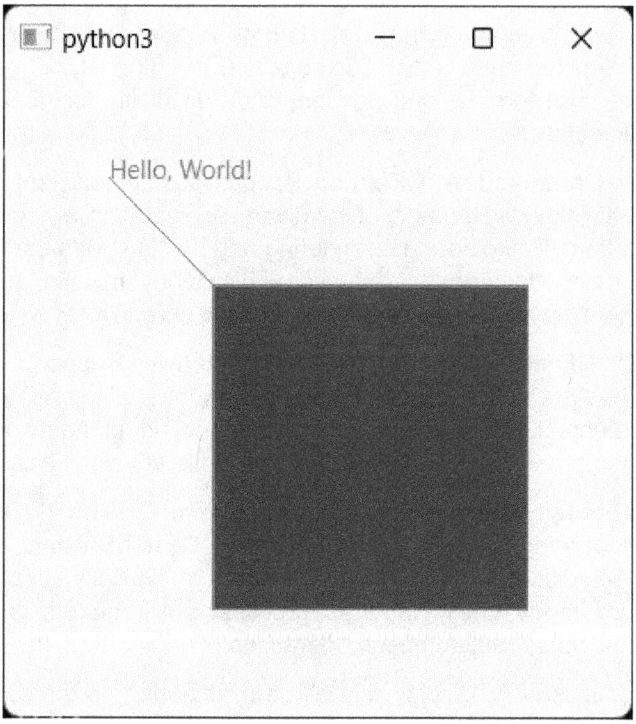

QPixmap

QPixmap is a class in PyQt6 that represents a graphic pixmap, which is a rectangular image or graphic. It is used to handle pixel-based images and provides methods for loading, creating, and manipulating pixmaps.

Should I use QPixmap or QImage?

QPixmap and QImage are both classes in PyQt6 used for handling images, but they have some differences in their functionality and usage.

Representation: **QPixmap** represents an image or pixmap that is optimized for display on the screen. It is designed to efficiently store and render pixel-based images, making it suitable for use with widgets and graphical user interfaces. **QImage**, on the other hand, represents a generic image that can be used for various purposes, including pixel manipulation, file I/O, and more.

Pixel Format: **QPixmap** uses a platform-specific pixel format optimized for display, which means it may not support all pixel formats or be suitable for extensive pixel manipulation. **QImage**, on the other hand, supports a wide range of pixel formats and provides more flexibility for direct pixel access and manipulation.

Display Optimisation: **QPixmap** is optimised for efficient display on the screen. It takes advantage of hardware acceleration and platform-specific optimisations to provide fast rendering and display updates. **QImage**, being more generic, does not have the same display optimisation and may require additional steps to display it efficiently on the screen.

File I/O: **QImage** provides more comprehensive support for reading and writing image files in various formats, including reading and writing individual pixel values. **QPixmap**, on the other hand, is primarily focused on in-memory representation and display, and its file I/O capabilities are limited.

Compatibility: QPixmap is often used directly with PyQt6 widgets for displaying images, such as **QLabel** or **QPushButton**, as it provides optimised display capabilities. **QImage** is typically used when more advanced image manipulation or processing is required, or when working with non-display-related image operations.

QPixmap is optimised for display and efficient rendering on the screen, making it suitable for use with PyQt6 widgets and graphical user interfaces. **QImage** provides more flexibility, supporting various pixel formats and offering more extensive image manipulation capabilities. It is often used for non-display-related image operations or advanced pixel manipulation tasks.

Syntax:

Load the required modules

from PyQt6.QtGui import QPixmap

Load from an image file

pixmap = QPixmap("path/to/image.png") # Load a pixmap from an image file

or define an empty Pixmap

pixmap = QPixmap(100, 100) # Create an empty pixmap with specified width and height

Methods:

load(fileName: str, format: str = None, flags: Union[QIODevice.OpenMode, QFlags[QIODevice.OpenModeFlag]] = QIODevice.OpenModeFlag.ReadOnly) -> bool	Loads an image from a file specified by fileName and returns True if successful. Optionally, you can specify the format of the image to be loaded.
isNull() -> bool	Returns True if the QPixmap is null, i.e., it does not contain any image data.
size() -> QSize	Returns the size of the pixmap as a QSize object.
width() -> int	Returns the width of the pixmap.
height() -> int	Returns the height of the pixmap.
scaled(width: int, height: int, aspectRatioMode: Qt.AspectRatioMode = Qt.AspectRatioMode.IgnoreAspectRatio, transformMode: Qt.TransformationMode = Qt.TransformationMode.FastTransformation) -> QPixmap	Returns a scaled copy of the pixmap with the specified width and height. You can also specify the aspectRatioMode and transformMode for scaling.
scaledToWidth(width: int, aspectRatioMode: Qt.AspectRatioMode = Qt.AspectRatioMode.IgnoreAspectRatio) -> QPixmap	Returns a scaled copy of the pixmap with the specified width, maintaining the aspect ratio. You can also specify the aspectRatioMode for scaling.

scaledToHeight(height: int, aspectRatioMode: Qt.AspectRatioMode = Qt.AspectRatioMode.IgnoreAspectRatio) -> QPixmap	Returns a scaled copy of the pixmap with the specified height, maintaining the aspect ratio. You can also specify the aspectRatioMode for scaling.
copy(rect: QRect = ...) -> QPixmap	Returns a copy of the pixmap, optionally specifying a rect to limit the copied area.
save(fileName: str, format: str = None, quality: int = -1) -> bool	Saves the pixmap to a file specified by fileName using the specified format. Optionally, you can specify the quality of the image.
toImage() -> QImage	Converts the pixmap to a **QImage** object.
fill(color: Union[QColor, Qt.GlobalColor])	Fills the pixmap with the specified colour.

Drawing on a QPixmap: You can draw on a **QPixmap** using various methods provided by **QPainter**, such as drawLine(), drawText(), or drawPixmap(). These methods allow you to add graphical elements or perform custom drawing on the pixmap.

Example:

```
painter = QPainter(pixmap)
painter.drawLine(0, 0, 100, 100)
painter.drawText(50, 50, "Hello, World!")
painter.end()
```

Resizing a QPixmap: You can resize a QPixmap using the **scaled()** or **scaledToWidth() / scaledToHeight()** methods. These methods allow you to scale the pixmap to a desired size while maintaining its aspect ratio.

Example:

```
pixmap = pixmap.scaled(200, 200)  # Scale the pixmap to a specific width
and height

pixmap = pixmap.scaledToWidth(300)  # Scale the pixmap to a specific
width, maintaining aspect ratio

pixmap = pixmap.scaledToHeight(150)  # Scale the pixmap to a specific
```

```
height, maintaining aspect ratio
```

Converting QPixmap to QImage: You can convert a **QPixmap** to a **QImage** using the **toImage()** method. **QImage** is another class in PyQt6 that represents an image.

Example:

```
image = pixmap.toImage()
```

Displaying a QPixmap: You can display a **QPixmap** on various PyQt6 widgets, such as **QLabel**, **QPushButton**, or **QGraphicsView**. Each widget provides a method or property to set the pixmap and display it.

Example:

```
from PyQt6.QtWidgets import QLabel

label = QLabel()
label.setPixmap(pixmap)
```

And an example showing a picture of a car on a label:

```
from PyQt6.QtWidgets import QApplication, QLabel, QVBoxLayout, QWidget
from PyQt6.QtGui import QPixmap
import sys

app = QApplication(sys.argv)

window = QWidget()
layout = QVBoxLayout(window)

label = QLabel()
pixmap = QPixmap("car.png")
label.setPixmap(pixmap)

layout.addWidget(label)
window.show()

sys.exit(app.exec())
```

Output:

QProgressBar

A widget that displays the progress of an operation. The **QProgressBar** class provides a visual component that represents the progress of a lengthy operation. It is commonly used to indicate the progress of tasks such as file downloads, data processing, or any operation that has a measurable progress.

Here are some key points about **QProgressBar**:

Visual Representation: QProgressBar displays a bar that fills up gradually to represent the progress of an operation. By default, it shows a continuous bar, but you can also configure it to display discrete values.

Value Range: The progress bar has a minimum and maximum value that define the range of the progress. As the operation progresses, you update the value of the progress bar to reflect the current progress.

Text Display: QProgressBar can optionally display text indicating the progress as a percentage or with a custom format. You can configure the text to be shown above or inside the progress bar.

Orientation: QProgressBar can be oriented horizontally or vertically, depending on the desired visual layout.

Appearance Customisation: QProgressBar provides several properties and methods to customise its appearance. You can set colours, text styles, text alignment, and control the animation behavior.

Syntax:

Import the required modules:

from PyQt6.QtWidgets import QProgressBar

Create a QProgressBar and set options such as range

progress_bar = QProgressBar()

progress_bar.setRange(0, 100)

Here are some of the commonly used methods:

setValue(value: int)	Sets the current value of the progress bar.
value() -> int	Returns the current value of the progress bar.
setRange(minimum: int, maximum: int)	Sets the minimum and maximum values of the progress bar range.
minimum() -> int	Returns the minimum value of the progress bar range.

maximum() -> int	Returns the maximum value of the progress bar range.
reset()	Resets the progress bar to its initial state (minimum value).
setTextVisible(visible: bool)	Sets whether the progress bar should display text.
isTextVisible() -> bool	Returns whether the progress bar displays text.
setFormat(format: str)	Sets the format of the text displayed on the progress bar.
format() -> str	Returns the current text format of the progress bar.
setAlignment(alignment: QtCore.Qt.AlignmentFlag)	Sets the alignment of the text displayed on the progress bar.
alignment() -> QtCore.Qt.AlignmentFlag	Returns the alignment of the progress bar text.
setOrientation(orientation: QtCore.Qt.Orientation)	Sets the orientation of the progress bar (horizontal or vertical).
orientation() -> QtCore.Qt.Orientation	Returns the current orientation of the progress bar.
setStyleSheet(styleSheet: str)	Sets the style sheet for customizing the appearance of the progress bar.
text() -> str	Returns the current text displayed on the progress bar.
setTextDirection(direction: QProgressBar.Direction)	Sets the direction in which the text is displayed on the progress bar.
textDirection() -> QProgressBar.Direction	Returns the current direction of the progress bar text.
setInvertedAppearance(inverted: bool)	Sets whether the progress bar should have an inverted appearance.

invertedAppearance() -> bool	Returns whether the progress bar has an inverted appearance.

Example:

```
from PyQt6.QtWidgets import QApplication, QWidget, QProgressBar,
QVBoxLayout, QLabel
from PyQt6.QtCore import QTimer

# Create a QApplication instance
app = QApplication([])

# Create a QMainWindow
window = QWidget()

# create a layout
my_layout = QVBoxLayout()

label1=QLabel("This is a QProgressBar")
label2=QLabel("Counting up to 100%")

# Create a QProgressBar and set its range
progress_bar = QProgressBar()
progress_bar.setRange(0, 100)

# Add the widgets to the layout
my_layout.addWidget(label1)
my_layout.addWidget(progress_bar)
my_layout.addWidget(label2)

# Set the main layout of the window
window.setLayout(my_layout)

value = 0

def update_progress():
        value = progress_bar.value()
        value += 1
        progress_bar.setValue(value)

timer = QTimer()
timer.timeout.connect(update_progress)
timer.start(100)  # Update every 0.1 second
```

```
# Show the main window
window.show()

# Start the application event loop
app.exec()
```

Output:

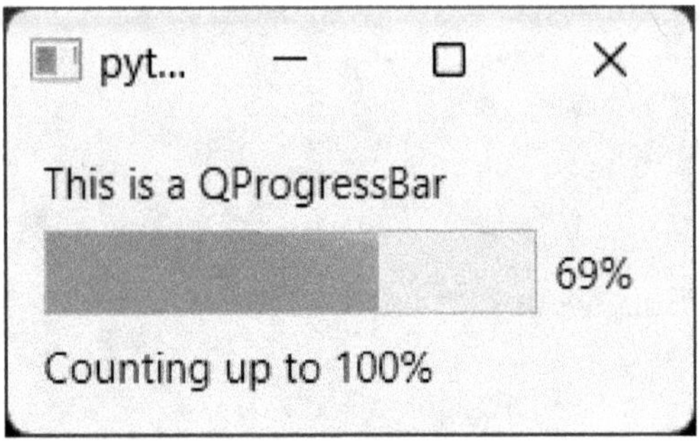

QProgressDialog

QProgressDialog is a dialog widget that provides a graphical representation of the progress of a long-running operation. It is commonly used to show the progress of tasks such as file downloads, data processing, or any operation that takes significant time to complete.

QProgressDialog has the following key features:

- It displays a progress bar that visually represents the progress of the operation.
- The progress bar can be updated to reflect the current progress value.
- It can display an optional label to provide additional information or description of the ongoing operation.
- QProgressDialog can be configured to be modal or non-modal. When modal, it blocks user interaction with other windows until it is closed.
- It can be set to automatically close when the operation reaches completion or can be manually closed by the user.

Syntax:

Import required modules

from PyQt6.QtWidgets import QApplication, QProgressDialog

from PyQt6.QtCore import Qt

create the progress dialog

progress_dialog = QProgressDialog("Downloading...", "Cancel", 0, 100)

set options eg:

progress_dialog.setWindowTitle("Progress")

Automatically close when progress reaches maximum

progress_dialog.setAutoClose(True)

Set as modal dialog

progress_dialog.setWindowModality(Qt.WindowModality.ApplicationModal)

Methods:

setRange(minimum: int, maximum: int)	Sets the minimum and maximum values for the progress bar.
setValue(value: int)	Sets the current value of the progress bar.
setLabelText(text: str)	Sets the text shown in the dialog's label.

setCancelButtonText(text: str)	Sets the text for the Cancel button.
setAutoClose(enable: bool)	Sets whether the dialog should automatically close when the progress reaches its maximum value.
setAutoReset(enable: bool)	Sets whether the dialog should automatically reset when the progress reaches its maximum value.
setCancelButton(button: QPushButton)	Sets the Cancel button for the dialog.
setWindowModality(modality: Qt.WindowModality)	Sets the window modality for the dialog.
exec()	Displays the progress dialog and starts the event loop.
wasCanceled() -> bool	Returns True if the user clicked the Cancel button, indicating cancellation of the operation.

Example:

```
from PyQt6.QtWidgets import QApplication, QProgressDialog,
QVBoxLayout, QPushButton, QDialog, QStyle
from PyQt6.QtCore import Qt, QTimer
import sys

app = QApplication(sys.argv)

progress_dialog = QProgressDialog()
progress_dialog.setLabelText("Processing...")
progress_dialog.setRange(0, 100)
progress_dialog.setAutoClose(False)
progress_dialog.setAutoReset(False)
progress_dialog.setWindowModality(Qt.WindowModality.ApplicationModal)

counter = 0

def update_progress():
    global counter
```

```
        counter += 1
        progress_dialog.setValue(counter)
        if counter >= 100:
            timer.stop()
            progress_dialog.setAutoClose(False)
            progress_dialog.setLabelText("Processing Complete")
            progress_dialog.setCancelButton(None)

    timer = QTimer()
    timer.timeout.connect(update_progress)
    timer.start(100)

    # Create a layout for the dialog
    layout = QVBoxLayout()
    layout.addWidget(progress_dialog)

    # Create a dialog and set the layout
    dialog = QDialog()
    dialog.setLayout(layout)

    # Center the dialog on the screen
    dialog.setGeometry(
        QStyle.alignedRect(
            Qt.LayoutDirection.LeftToRight,
            Qt.AlignmentFlag.AlignCenter,
            dialog.size(),
            app.primaryScreen().availableGeometry()
        )
    )

    # Show the dialog
    dialog.exec()

    sys.exit(app.exec())
```

Output:

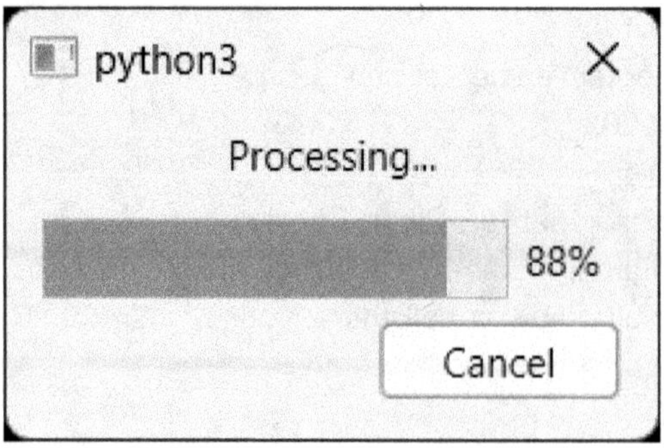
python3
Processing...
88%
Cancel

QPushButton

QPushButton is a widget that represents a clickable button. It is commonly used to trigger actions or perform specific tasks when clicked by the user.

Syntax:

Import the required modules

from PyQt6.QtWidgets import QApplication, QPushButton, QWidget

create a QPushButton instance with required text

my_button = QPushButton("Click me!")

optionally add a 'tool tip' to be shown when the mouse hovers over

my_button.setToolTip("This is a tooltip") # Set the tooltip text

If you want the button to do something when it is clicked:

my_button.clicked.connect(button_clicked)

button_clicked is the name of a function called when the button is clicked

def button_clicked():

print("Button clicked!")

Here are some commonly used methods associated with **QPushButton**:

setText(text: str)	Sets the text displayed on the button.
text() -> str	Returns the current text displayed on the button.
clicked.connect(slot)	Connects a slot function to the clicked signal of the button. The slot function is called when the button is clicked.
setEnabled(enabled: bool)	Enables or disables the button. If enabled is True, the button can be interacted with; if False, it is greyed out and cannot be clicked.
isEnabled() -> bool	Returns True if the button is enabled, False otherwise.
setDefault(default: bool)	Sets the button as the default button for a dialog or form. The default button is activated when the user presses the Enter key.

setAutoDefault(autoDefault: bool)	Sets the button as the auto-default button. The auto-default button is activated when the user presses the Enter key, but only if no other widget in the window has focus.
setToolTip(tooltip: str)	Sets the tooltip text that appears when the mouse hovers over the button.
setStyleSheet(stylesheet: str)	Applies a stylesheet to customise the appearance of the button.
setCheckable(checkable: bool)	Enables or disables the button's checkable state. If checkable is True, the button can be toggled between checked and unchecked states.
setChecked(checked: bool)	Sets the checked state of the button. Applicable only if the button is checkable.
isChecked() -> bool	Returns True if the button is checked, False otherwise.
setIcon(icon: QIcon)	Sets an icon for the button.
setIconSize(size: QSize)	Sets the size of the icon displayed on the button.

Example:

```
from PyQt6.QtWidgets import QApplication, QHBoxLayout, QPushButton,
QWidget
from PyQt6.QtGui import QColor
import sys

def toggle_button_state():
    button = app.focusWidget()
    if isinstance(button, QPushButton):
        if button.text() == "OFF":
            button.setStyleSheet("background-color: green; color: white;")
            button.setText("ON")
        else:
            button.setStyleSheet("background-color: red; color: white;")
            button.setText("OFF")
```

```
app = QApplication(sys.argv)

window = QWidget()
layout = QHBoxLayout(window)

button1 = QPushButton("OFF")
button1.setStyleSheet("background-color: red; color: white;")
button1.clicked.connect(toggle_button_state)

button2 = QPushButton("OFF")
button2.setStyleSheet("background-color: red; color: white;")
button2.clicked.connect(toggle_button_state)

button3 = QPushButton("OFF")
button3.setStyleSheet("background-color: red; color: white;")
button3.clicked.connect(toggle_button_state)

layout.addWidget(button1)
layout.addWidget(button2)
layout.addWidget(button3)

window.show()

sys.exit(app.exec())
```

Output:

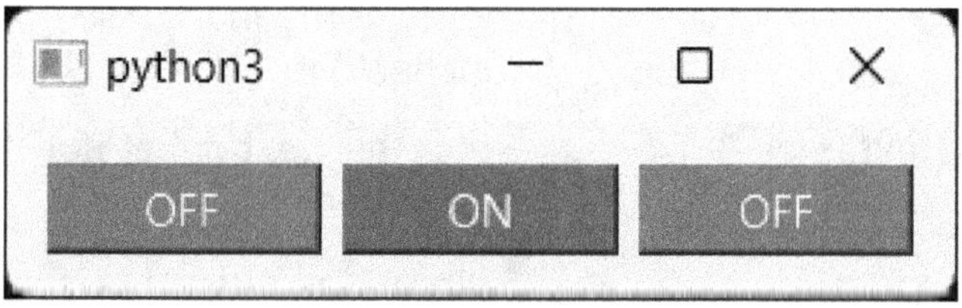

The 'OFF' buttons are white text on red and the 'ON' buttons are white text on green.

QRadioButton

QRadioButton is a widget that represents a selectable button with an exclusive choice. It is commonly used to present a set of options where only one option can be selected at a time.

Each QRadioButton instance represents a single option within a group of radio buttons. When one radio button is selected, the previously selected radio button within the same group is automatically deselected.

Syntax:

Import the required modules

from PyQt6.QtWidgets import QApplication, QRadioButton, QWidget

Create an instance of QRadioButton:

radio_button1 = QRadioButton("Option 1")

radio_button2 = QRadioButton("Option 2")

By default, radio buttons are not selected. You can set the initial selection state using the setChecked() method:

radio_button1.setChecked(True)

Here are some commonly used methods associated with QRadioButton:

isChecked() -> bool	Returns True if the radio button is currently selected (checked), False otherwise.
setChecked(checked: bool)	Sets the selection state of the radio button. Pass True to select (check) the button, and False to deselect (uncheck) it.
setText(text: str)	Sets the text label for the radio button.
text() -> str	Returns the current text label of the radio button.
setEnabled(enabled: bool)	Enables or disables the radio button. If enabled is True, the radio button can be interacted with; if False, it is greyed out and cannot be selected.
setToolTip(tooltip: str)	Sets the tooltip text that appears when the mouse hovers over the radio button.

setAutoExclusive(exclusive: bool)	Enables or disables the auto-exclusive behavior of the radio button. When auto-exclusive is enabled (True), selecting one radio button automatically deselects others within the same parent widget. By default, auto-exclusive is enabled.
isChecked() -> bool	Returns True if the radio button is selected (checked), False otherwise.
toggle()	Toggles the selection state of the radio button. If it is currently selected, it will be deselected, and vice versa.
setIcon(icon: QIcon)	Sets an icon for the radio button.
setIconSize(size: QSize)	Sets the size of the icon displayed on the radio button.

Example:

```
from PyQt6.QtWidgets import QApplication, QVBoxLayout, QRadioButton,
QLabel, QWidget
import sys

def update_label():
    selected_option = ""
    if radio_button1.isChecked():
        selected_option = radio_button1.text()
    elif radio_button2.isChecked():
        selected_option = radio_button2.text()
    label.setText("Selected option: " + selected_option)

# Create the application
app = QApplication(sys.argv)

# Create a QWidget as the main window
window = QWidget()
window.setWindowTitle("QRadioButton Example")

# Create a QVBoxLayout for the window
```

```
layout = QVBoxLayout(window)

# Create two QRadioButtons
radio_button1 = QRadioButton("Option 1")
radio_button2 = QRadioButton("Option 2")

# Create a QLabel to display the selected option
label = QLabel("Selected option: ")

# Connect the radio buttons to the update_label function
radio_button1.toggled.connect(update_label)
radio_button2.toggled.connect(update_label)

# Add the radio buttons and label to the layout
layout.addWidget(radio_button1)
layout.addWidget(radio_button2)
layout.addWidget(label)

# Show the window
window.show()

# Start the event loop
sys.exit(app.exec())
```

Output:

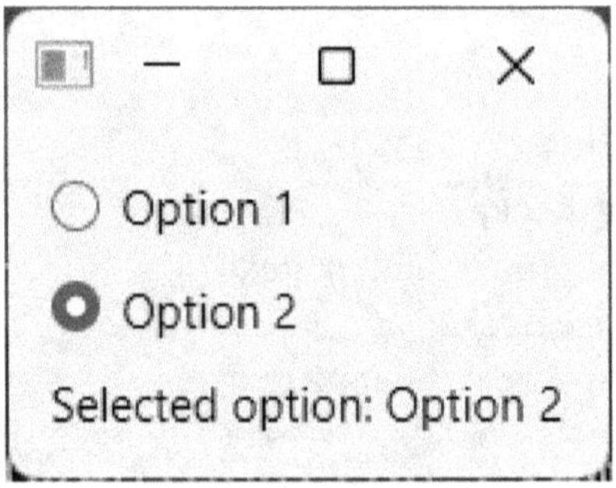

QSize

QSize is a class that represents a two-dimensional size or dimension. It is typically used to specify the width and height of graphical elements such as widgets, images, or layouts.

Here are some key points about **QSize**:

- **QSize** objects are created using the constructor **QSize(width: int, height: int).** The width and height parameters specify the dimensions of the size.
- The width and height of a QSize can be accessed and modified using the **width()** and **height()** methods, respectively. For example, **size.width()** returns the width of the **QSize** object.
- **QSize** objects can be compared using equality operators (==, !=) to check if they have the same dimensions.
- Arithmetic operations such as addition (+) and subtraction (-) can be performed on **QSize** objects to combine or adjust their dimensions.
- **QSize** objects can be used to set the size of graphical elements such as widgets or images. For example, when creating a widget, you can specify its size using a **QSize** object.
- The **QSize** class also provides methods for convenience operations such as scaling (scaled()), transposing (transposed()), and converting to a string representation (toString()).

Syntax:

from PyQt6.QtCore import QSize

size = QSize(width, height)

Methods:

width() -> int	Returns the width of the QSize object as an integer.
height() -> int	Returns the height of the QSize object as an integer.
setWidth(width: int) -> None	Sets the width of the QSize object to the specified value.
setHeight(height: int) -> None	Sets the height of the QSize object to the specified value.
isNull() -> bool	Checks if the QSize object is null, meaning both width and height are zero.

isEmpty() -> bool	Checks if the QSize object is empty, meaning either width or height is zero or negative.
isValid() -> bool	Checks if the QSize object is valid, meaning both width and height are greater than zero.
transpose() -> QSize	Returns a new QSize object with the width and height swapped.
scaled(swidth: int, sheight: int, aspectRatioMode: Qt.AspectRatioMode = Qt.AspectRatioMode.IgnoreAspectRatio) -> QSize	Returns a new QSize object that is scaled by the specified width and height factors. You can also specify an aspect ratio mode for handling the scaling.
expandedTo(other: QSize) -> QSize	Returns a new QSize object that is expanded to the maximum width and height of either the current size or the specified other size.
boundedTo(other: QSize) -> QSize	Returns a new QSize object that is bounded by the minimum width and height of either the current size or the specified other size.
isEmpty() -> bool	Checks if the QSize object is empty, meaning either width or height is zero or negative.

Example (note that long lines have wrapped around in this example):

```
from PyQt6.QtCore import QSize, Qt

# Create an original QSize object
original_size = QSize(800, 600)

# Scale the size to a new width and height using different aspect ratio
modes
scaled_size_ignore = original_size.scaled(1920, 1080,
Qt.AspectRatioMode.IgnoreAspectRatio)
scaled_size_keep = original_size.scaled(1920, 1080,
Qt.AspectRatioMode.KeepAspectRatio)
scaled_size_fixed = original_size.scaled(1920, 1080,
Qt.AspectRatioMode.KeepAspectRatioByExpanding)

# Print the original and scaled sizes
print("Original Size:", original_size.width(), original_size.height())
print("Scaled Size (Ignore Aspect Ratio):", scaled_size_ignore.width(),
scaled_size_ignore.height())
print("Scaled Size (Keep Aspect Ratio):", scaled_size_keep.width(),
scaled_size_keep.height())
print("Scaled Size (Keep Aspect Ratio By Expanding):",
scaled_size_fixed.width(), scaled_size_fixed.height())
```

Output:

Original Size: 800 600

Scaled Size (Ignore Aspect Ratio): 1920 1080

Scaled Size (Keep Aspect Ratio): 1440 1080

Scaled Size (Keep Aspect Ratio By Expanding): 1920 1440

QSlider

QSlider is a widget that provides a horizontal or vertical slider control that allows the user to select a value within a specified range. It is commonly used to implement sliders or progress bars in graphical user interfaces.

QSlider has the following key features:

- It can be oriented horizontally or vertically based on the desired layout.
- The slider handle, also known as the thumb or slider grip, can be dragged by the user to change the selected value.
- It supports a range of values, specified by a minimum and maximum value.
- The current value of the slider can be retrieved or set programmatically.
- QSlider can display optional tick marks and labels to indicate specific values or intervals.

Syntax:

Import the necessary modules

from PyQt6.QtWidgets import QSlider

from PyQt6.QtCore import Qt

create the slider and set options

slider = QSlider(Qt.Orientation.Horizontal, parent)

slider.setGeometry(x, y, width, height)

slider.setRange(0, 100)

Methods:

setOrientation(orientation: Qt.Orientation)	Sets the orientation of the slider. The orientation parameter can be Qt.Orientation.Horizontal or Qt.Orientation.Vertical.
setRange(minimum: int, maximum: int)	Sets the minimum and maximum values for the slider range.
setValue(value: int)	Sets the current value of the slider.
value() -> int	Returns the current value of the slider.
setTickInterval(interval: int)	Sets the interval between tick marks.

setTickPosition(position : QSlider.TickPosition)	Sets the position of the tick marks. The position parameter can be QSlider.TickPosition.NoTicks, QSlider.TickPosition.TicksAbove, QSlider.TickPosition.TicksBelow, QSlider.TickPosition.TicksBothSides, or QSlider.TickPosition.TicksLeft.
setSingleStep(step: int)	Sets the single step value for the slider. The single step value determines the amount by which the slider's value changes when using arrow keys or clicking on the slider track.
setPageStep(step: int)	Sets the page step value for the slider. The page step value determines the amount by which the slider's value changes when using page up/page down keys or clicking on the slider track away from the handle.
setTracking(enable: bool)	Enables or disables slider tracking. When tracking is enabled, the valueChanged signal is emitted continuously while dragging the slider handle. When disabled, the signal is emitted only when the handle is released.

Example:

```
from PyQt6.QtWidgets import QApplication, QMainWindow, QSlider,
QLabel
from PyQt6.QtCore import Qt
import sys

app = QApplication(sys.argv)
app.setStyle("windows")
window = QMainWindow()
window.setGeometry(100, 100, 300, 200)

slider = QSlider(Qt.Orientation.Horizontal, window)
```

```
slider.setGeometry(50, 50, 200, 30)
slider.setRange(0, 100)
slider.setTickPosition(QSlider.TickPosition.TicksBothSides)
slider.setTickInterval(10)

label = QLabel(window)
label.setText("Selected Value: ")
label.setGeometry(50, 100, 200, 30)
label.setAlignment(Qt.AlignmentFlag.AlignCenter)

def on_slider_value_changed(value):
    label.setText(f"Selected Value: {value}")

slider.valueChanged.connect(on_slider_value_changed)

window.show()
sys.exit(app.exec())
```

Output (I changed the window style from the default "fusion" to "windows" so that it would be clearer in a greyscale print).:

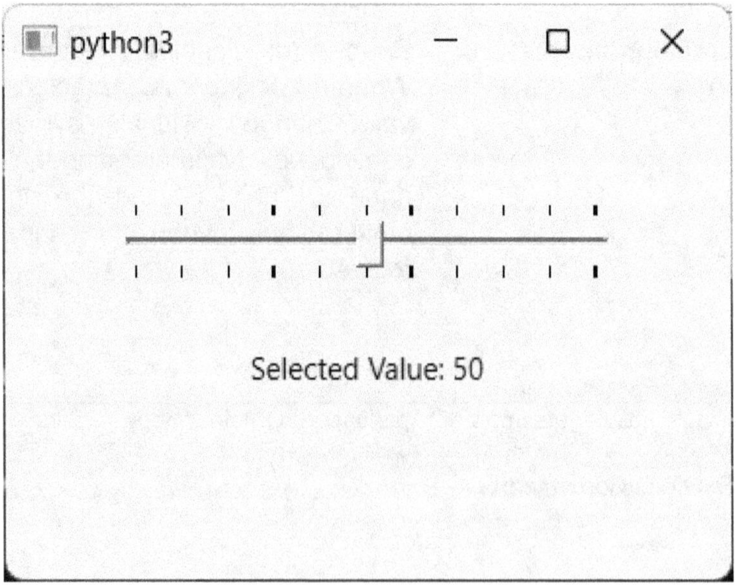

QStatusBar

QStatusBar is a class in that provides a horizontal bar at the bottom of a **QMainWindow** or a **QDialog** window to display messages or other status information about an application.

The **QStatusBar** widget can display temporary messages or permanent widgets. You can add permanent widgets such as buttons, progress bars, labels, and other widgets to the status bar, and these widgets will be displayed continuously. You can also show temporary messages that will appear briefly, and then disappear after a set amount of time.

Syntax:

my_status_bar = QStatusBar()

Methods:

showMessage(message: str, timeout: int = 0)	displays a temporary message in the status bar with the specified message string. The message will be shown for timeout milliseconds, or indefinitely if timeout is set to 0 (the default).
addPermanentWidget(widget: QWidget, stretch: int = 0)	adds a permanent widget to the right-hand side of the status bar. The widget argument is the widget to be added, and stretch is an optional integer value that specifies how much space the widget should take up in the status bar relative to other widgets. The default value of stretch is 0, meaning the widget will take up as much space as necessary.
addWidget(widget: QWidget, stretch: int = 0)	adds a widget to the status bar. The widget argument is the widget to be added, and stretch is an optional integer value that specifies how much space the widget should take up in the status bar relative to other widgets. The default value of stretch is 0, meaning the widget will take up as much space as necessary.

removeWidget(widget: QWidget)	removes the specified widget from the status bar.
clearMessage()	clears the current message displayed in the status bar.
clearPermanentWidgets()	removes all permanent widgets from the status bar.
currentMessage() -> str	returns the current message displayed in the status bar.

Here's an example of how to add a status bar

```
from PyQt6.QtWidgets import QApplication, QMainWindow, QStatusBar,
QPushButton

app = QApplication([])

# Create a main window
window = QMainWindow()
window.setWindowTitle('Status Bar Example')

# Create a status bar
status_bar = QStatusBar()
status_bar.showMessage('Ready')
window.setStatusBar(status_bar)

window.show()
app.exec()
```

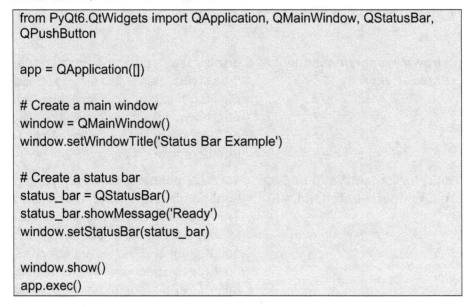

Output:

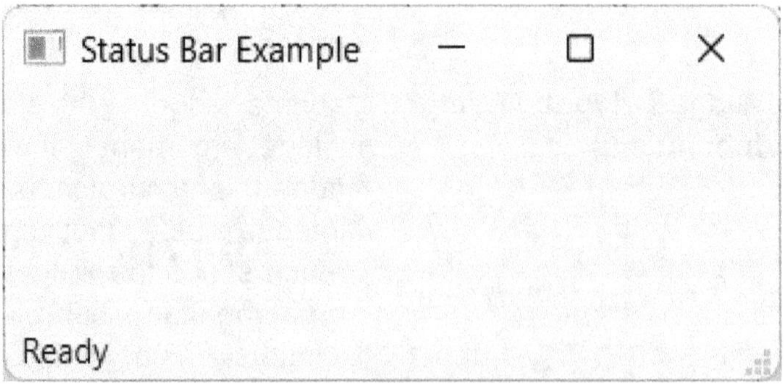

QSpinBox

QSpinBox is a widget that allows the user to select a numeric value from a range of values. It provides a simple way to select a value from a range using an up/down arrow button or by typing the value directly.

QSpinBox inherits from **QAbstractSpinBox** and is designed to handle integer and floating-point values. It provides a user interface for selecting an integer value from a range of values, which can be specified using the **setRange()** method.

QSpinBox also provides a number of other methods and signals for customizing its behavior and responding to changes in the selected value. For example, you can use the **setSingleStep()** method to specify the amount by which the value changes when the up/down arrow buttons are clicked, and you can use the **valueChanged** signal to respond to changes in the selected value. Here are a few of the methods used with **QSpinBox**:

setRange(bottom: int, top: int)	Sets the minimum and maximum values for the spin box.
setSingleStep(step: int)	Sets the amount by which the value changes when the up or down buttons are clicked.
setValue(value: int)	Sets the current value of the spin box.
value() -> int	Returns the current value of the spin box.
text() -> str	Returns the text representation of the current value of the spin box.
cleanText() -> str	Returns the text representation of the current value of the spin box without any formatting or prefix/suffix text.
setPrefix(text: str)	Sets the prefix text to display before the value.
setSuffix(text: str)	Sets the suffix text to display after the value.
setWrapping(enable: bool)	Sets whether the spin box wraps around from the maximum value to the minimum value, and vice versa.
setAlignment(alignment: Qt.AlignmentFlag)	Sets the horizontal alignment of the spin box text.

Example:

```
from PyQt6.QtWidgets import QApplication, QMainWindow, QSpinBox,
QVBoxLayout, QWidget

app = QApplication([])
window = QMainWindow()
window.setWindowTitle('Spin Box Example')
window.setGeometry(100, 100, 300, 150)

spin_box = QSpinBox()
spin_box.setRange(0, 100)
spin_box.setSingleStep(1)
spin_box.setValue(50)

layout = QVBoxLayout()
layout.addWidget(spin_box)

widget = QWidget()
widget.setLayout(layout)

window.setCentralWidget(widget)
window.show()
app.exec()
```

Output:

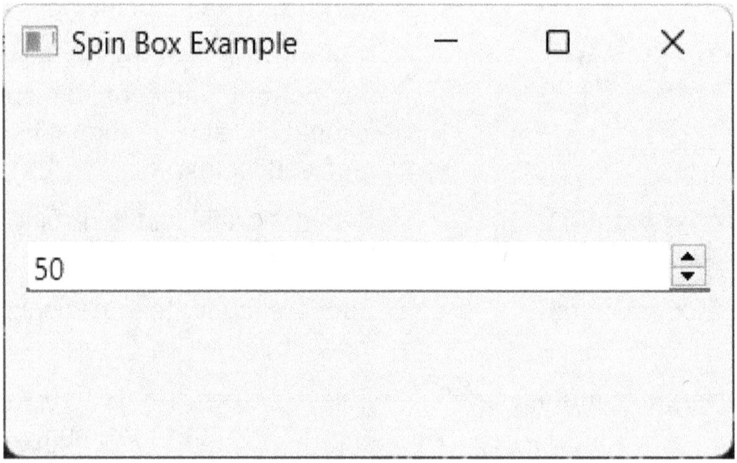

QTextEdit

QTextEdit is a widget in that allows users to edit and display formatted text over multiple lines. It provides a powerful and flexible editing environment, with support for a variety of text formats, styles, and formatting options. See also **QTextCursor** in the next section.

Feature of **QTextEdit** include::

Rich text editing: QTextEdit supports basic formatting such as bold, italic, underline, and strikethrough, as well as more advanced formatting such as font family and size, colour, alignment, and indentation.

HTML and plain text editing: QTextEdit can be used to edit both HTML and plain text. It also supports pasting text from other applications, including formatted text and images.

Undo and redo: QTextEdit provides undo and redo functionality, allowing users to easily undo and redo changes to the text.

Spell checking: QTextEdit includes built-in spell checking functionality, which can be enabled or disabled as needed.

Automatic formatting: QTextEdit can automatically format text as it is typed, such as automatically creating bulleted or numbered lists.

Images and hyperlinks: QTextEdit supports embedding images and hyperlinks in the text, and allows users to click on hyperlinks to open web pages or other documents.

Printing: QTextEdit can be printed directly and supports options such as page breaks and margins.

Methods of **QTextEdit** include:

setPlainText(text: str) and toPlainText() -> str	Set or retrieve the plain text content of the QTextEdit widget.
setHtml(html: str) and toHtml() -> str	Set or retrieve the HTML content of the QTextEdit widget.
setReadOnly(readOnly: bool)	Set whether the QTextEdit widget is read-only.
undo() and redo()	Perform undo or redo operations on the content of the QTextEdit widget.
copy(), cut(), and paste()	Copy, cut, or paste text content to or from the clipboard.
setFont(font: QFont)	Set the font used for the text in the QTextEdit widget.

setTextColor(color: QColor)	Set the colour used for the text in the QTextEdit widget.

Example:

```
from PyQt6.QtWidgets import QApplication, QMainWindow, QTextEdit
import sys

app = QApplication(sys.argv)
window = QMainWindow()
window.setWindowTitle('Text Edit Example')
window.setGeometry(100, 100, 300, 150)

text_edit = QTextEdit()
window.setCentralWidget(text_edit)

window.show()
sys.exit(app.exec())
```

Output:

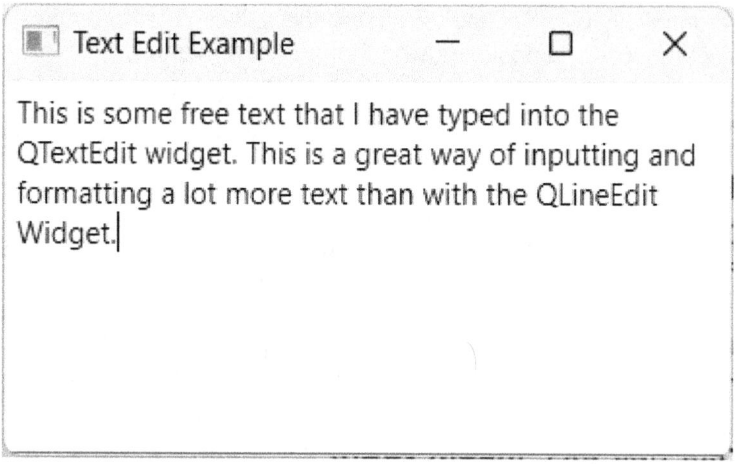

QTextCursor

QTextCursor is a class in that represents a cursor in a **QTextEdit** widget. The **QTextCursor** class provides several methods for manipulating the cursor's position and text selection in the widget.

from PyQt6.QtGui import QTextCursor

The term "anchor" is used in the context of **QTextCursor** to refer to one end of a selected range of text.

When you select a range of text in a **QTextEdit** widget, the QTextCursor object representing the selection has two points of reference: the anchor and the position. The position is the current location of the cursor, while the anchor is the opposite end of the selected range.

The anchor can be thought of as the fixed point of the selection, while the position can move around freely. When you move the **QTextCursor** using the **movePosition()** method, you are moving the position of the cursor, but the anchor remains fixed, resulting in the selection changing in size.

You can set the anchor of a **QTextCursor** object explicitly using the **setPosition()** method, or implicitly by selecting text using the select() method. Once the anchor is set, you can access its position using the **anchor()** method.

Here are some of the most commonly used methods for **QTextCursor**:

position()	returns the current position of the cursor within the document.
setPosition(position)	sets the position of the cursor to the given position.
movePosition(operation, mode=QTextCursor.MoveAnchor, n=1)	moves the cursor by n characters or to a specific position, depending on the operation and mode parameters. The operation parameter should be one of the constants defined in the QTextCursor.MoveOperation enum (e.g. QTextCursor.Left, QTextCursor.Right, QTextCursor.Up, QTextCursor.Down, etc.).
insertText(text)	inserts the given text at the current position of the cursor.
removeSelectedText()	removes the currently selected text, if any.

hasSelection()	returns True if there is currently selected text, and False otherwise.
selectedText()	returns the currently selected text, if any.
select(selection)	selects the given selection, which should be an instance of the **QTextCursor** class.
selectedText()	returns the currently selected text, if any.
selectedTableCells()	returns the table cells currently selected by the cursor, if any.
selectedTable()	returns the table currently selected by the cursor, if any.

The Anchor

In the context of PyQt6 and **QTextCursor**, the anchor refers to the position where the user started the selection of text.

When a user selects text in a **QTextEdit** widget, the anchor is the position of the cursor when the user started the selection. The position of the cursor when the user finishes the selection is referred to as the position of the cursor.

The **QTextCursor.anchor()** method returns the anchor position of the cursor. The **QTextCursor.position()** method returns the current position of the cursor.

These two positions are useful for selecting a range of text, such as when using the **QTextCursor.selectedText()** method to retrieve the text that is currently selected.

As you can see, the **QTextCursor** offers some powerful options to manipulate the text in a **QTextEdit** widget.

There are a couple of ways in which you can format the text in a **QTextEdit** Widget and I will provide a couple of examples for these:

> **QTextCharFormat** (just below) allows text to be formatted using **QFont** (*see later section*)

HTML just as we can insert plain text into a **QTextEdit** widget we can also insert **HTML** formatted text along with standard HTML tags e.g. **window.textEdit.setHtml(text)** I will provide an example of this further below.

QTextCharFormat

As you can see, the **QTextCursor** offers some powerful options to manipulate the text in a **QTextEdit** widget.

It provides a way to define various text attributes such as font, font size, font colour, bold, italic, underline, strike-through, and more.

QTextCharFormat can be used to format both plain text and rich text. It is a lightweight object that stores character formatting properties and can be applied to selected text in a text edit or used as the default format for new text.

The properties of a **QTextCharFormat** object can be set using the various set methods provided by the class. For example, to set the font size to 12, you can use **setFontSize(12).** Similarly, to set the font colour to red, you can use **setForeground(Qt.red).**

QTextCharFormat can be applied to selected text in a **QTextEdit** using the **mergeCharFormat** or **mergeCurrentCharFormat** methods. The **mergeCharFormat** method applies the format to the entire selection, while the **mergeCurrentCharFormat** method applies the format only to the current character or the characters being typed.

This example shows a little about both cursor control and changing the text format:

```
from PyQt6.QtWidgets import QApplication, QTextEdit
from PyQt6.QtGui import QTextCursor, QFont, QTextCharFormat

# create a QApplication instance
app = QApplication([])

# create a QTextEdit widget
text_edit = QTextEdit()
text_edit.setPlainText("This is just some sample text")

# set the cursor position and select some text
cursor = text_edit.textCursor()
cursor.setPosition(18)
cursor.movePosition(QTextCursor.MoveOperation.Right,
QTextCursor.MoveMode.KeepAnchor, 6)
text_edit.setTextCursor(cursor)
```

```
# print some attributes of the cursor
print(f"Cursor position: {cursor.position()}")
print(f"Anchor Position:{cursor.anchor()}")
print(f"Selected text: {cursor.selectedText()}")
print(f"Has selection: {cursor.hasSelection()}")

# set highlighted text to bold by merging current format with bold
char_format = text_edit.currentCharFormat()
bold_format = QTextCharFormat()
bold_format.setFontWeight(QFont.Weight.Bold)
text_edit.mergeCurrentCharFormat(bold_format)

# show the QTextEdit widget
text_edit.show()

# start the QApplication event loop
app.exec()
```

Console output:

Cursor position: 24
Anchor Position:18
Selected text: sample
Has selection: True

Screen Output:

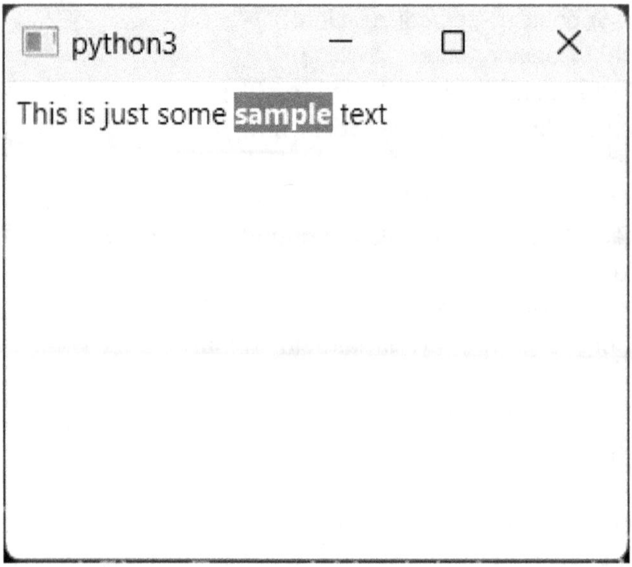

This shows that the text “This is just some sample text” has been placed, the cursor is then set at position 18 (the ‘s’) and is then moved right 6 positions to location 24. Because we have used the **KeepAnchor** option, the anchor stays at position 18 and the text from 18 to 24 (the word ‘sample’) is highlighted (see above). The output printed to the console (see above) is useful for troubleshooting purposes to confirm this. The pic below show the screen when the word sample is no longer highlighted.

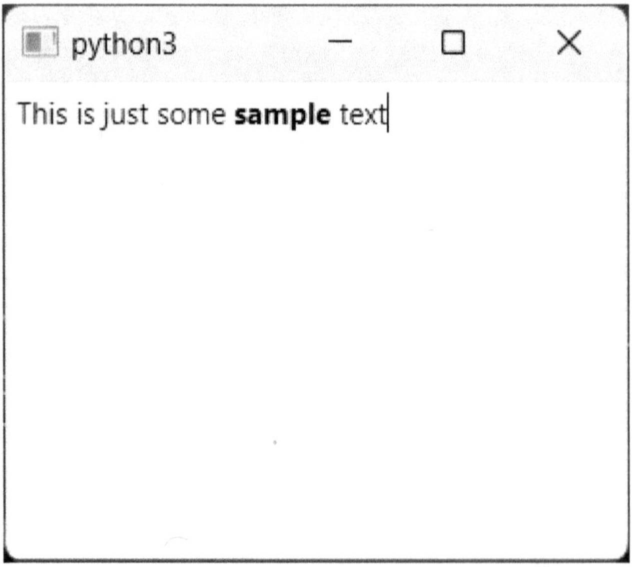

QTextEdit with HTML

In this example the user is invited to select a directory containing **MS Excel** spreadsheet files using the **QFileDialog**. The program then lists the filename of these files in a **QTextEdit** widget along with the value of the first non-empty cell and its cell reference. Both the filename and the value of the first cell are output in bold by using the **<b> text </b> HTML** tags.

This example has had the user interface designed using in **Qt Designer** and saved as **excelui.ui**. The three widgets used are a **QLabel, QPushButton** and a **QTextEdit.** In the code, these widgets are referred to by their **objectNames** from **Qt Designer** which are **pushButton** and **textEdit** (the label is not referenced). The text to be output is stored in a string variable called result and is into the **QTextEdit** using:

main_window.textEdit.setHtml(result)

The result string is:

result += f"<p>File: <b>{filename}, </b> First cell: <b>{cell.value}</b> ({cell.coordinate})"

So you will see the HTML tags for:

Paragraph: <p>
Bold: <b> to </b>
Included in this text string.

Example:

```
import os
from PyQt6.QtWidgets import QApplication, QMainWindow, QWidget,
QFileDialog, QLabel, QPushButton, QTextEdit
from PyQt6 import uic # user interface converter
import openpyxl
                                   import sys

app = QApplication([])

main_window = uic.loadUi(r"c:\Users\paul_\excelui.ui")

# Define the function to handle the button click event
def select_dir():
   # Prompt the user to select a directory
   directory = QFileDialog.getExistingDirectory(main_window, "Select
Directory")
   result = ""
   for filename in os.listdir(directory): # Loop through each file in the
directory
```

```
        if filename.endswith('.xlsx'): # Check if file is an Excel file
            workbook = openpyxl.load_workbook(os.path.join(directory, filename)) # Load the workbook
            sheet = workbook.active
            for row in sheet.rows: # Loop through each row and column until a non-empty cell is found
                for cell in row:
                    if cell.value is not None:
                        result += f"<p>File: <b>{filename}, </b> First cell: <b>{cell.value}</b> ({cell.coordinate})"
                        break
                else:
                    continue
                break
    main_window.textEdit.setHtml(result) # Update the QTextEdit with the result

main_window.pushButton.clicked.connect(select_dir) # Connect the button click event to the function

main_window.show() # Show the main window

app.exec() # Run the application
```

QTextEdit Example using UIC File from Qt Designer

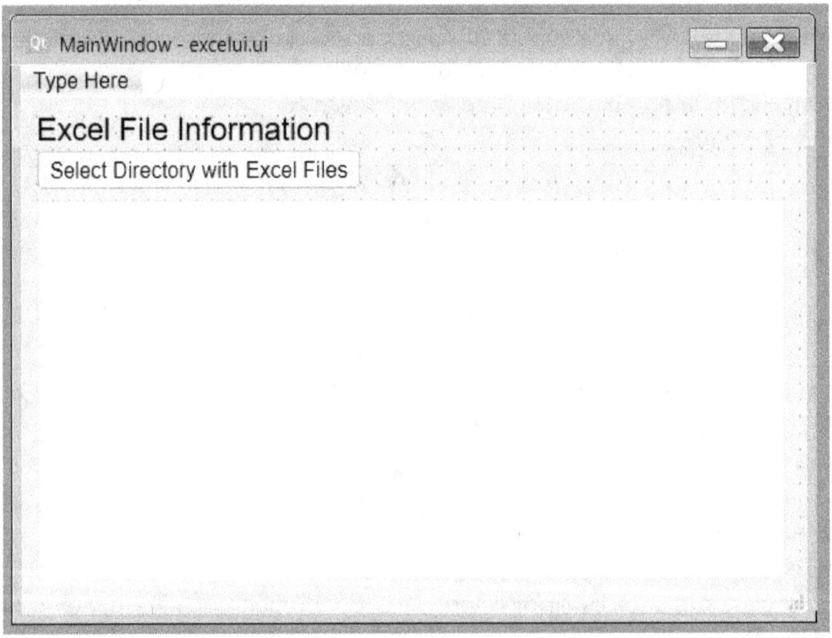

Output (showing text elements have been made **bold** using HTML).:

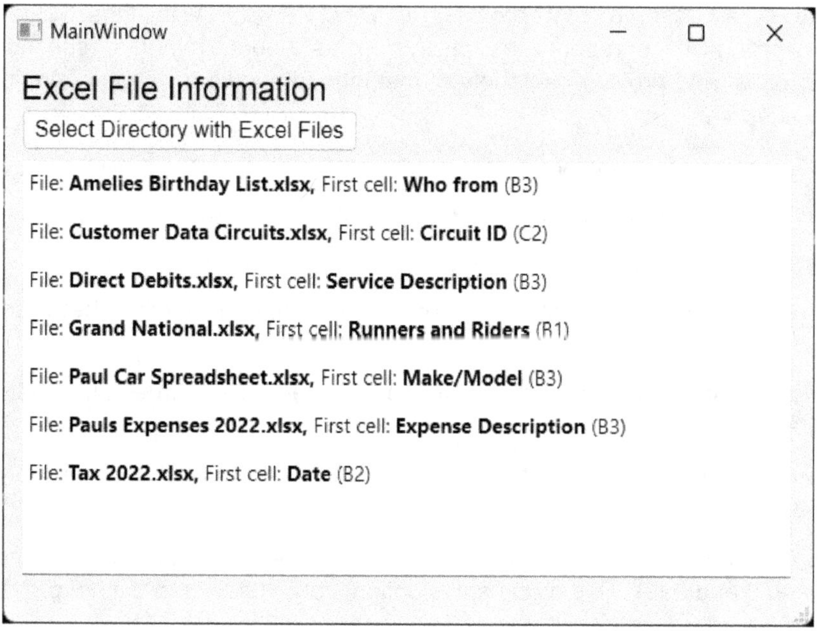

QTime

QTime is a class in that provides a way to work with time values in a Qt application. It represents a time value as hours, minutes, seconds, and milliseconds, and provides a variety of methods for working with and manipulating time values.

Syntax:

QTime(hour: int, minute: int, second: int, msec: int = 0)

This constructor takes four arguments:

hour: an integer value for the hour component of the time value (between 0 and 23).

minute: an integer value for the minute component of the time value (between 0 and 59).

second: an integer value for the second component of the time value (between 0 and 59).

msec (optional): an integer value for the millisecond component of the time value (between 0 and 999). This argument is optional and defaults to 0 if not provided.

Features include:

> **Time formatting**: QTime provides methods for formatting a time value as a string, with options for different formats, including 12-hour or 24-hour time, and with or without leading zeroes.
>
> **Time arithmetic**: QTime provides methods for performing arithmetic operations on time values, such as adding or subtracting a certain number of hours, minutes, seconds, or milliseconds.
>
> **Time comparisons:** QTime provides methods for comparing time values, such as checking whether one time is greater than or equal to another time.
>
> **Time parsing:** QTime provides methods for parsing a time value from a string, with options for different input formats.

Methods include:

currentTime() -> QTime	Return the current system time as a **QTime** object.
toString(format: str) -> str	Return the time value as a string formatted according to the given format string.
addHours(hours: int), addMinutes(minutes: int), addSeconds(seconds: int), addMSecs(msecs: int)	Add the given number of hours, minutes, seconds, or milliseconds to the time value.

hour() -> int, minute() -> int, second() -> int, msec() -> int	Return the hour, minute, second, or millisecond component of the time value.
isValid() -> bool	Return True if the time value is valid or False otherwise.
fromString(s: str, format: str) -> QTime	Parse the time value from the given string using the given format string. If the string is not a valid time, return an invalid QTime object.

Example:

```
from PyQt6.QtCore import QTime

time = QTime(15, 45, 30, 0)

print(time)
print(time.toString('hh:mm'))
```

Output:

PyQt6.QtCore.QTime(15, 45, 30)

15:45

The exact format of the output depends on the format string used, and that there are many different options for formatting the output of a QTime object using the **toString()** method

QTimeEdit

QTimeEdit is a widget in that allows the user to edit a time value. It displays the current time value as a formatted string and provides a drop-down menu that allows the user to adjust the time value by changing the hours, minutes, and seconds using up/down arrow buttons or by directly typing in the time value.

Here are some of the main features:

It inherits from **QDateTimeEdit**, which means that it shares many of the same properties and methods as **QDateTimeEdit**.

The time value is stored as a **QTime** object, which can be accessed using the **time()** method.

The format of the time value can be customised using the **setDisplayFormat()** method.

The range of valid time values can be limited using the **setMinimumTime()** and **setMaximumTime()** methods.

Syntax:

Import the required modules e.g.:

from PyQt6.QtWidgets import QApplication, QTimeEdit
from PyQt6.QtCore import QTime
Create a QTimeEdit widget and set options
time_edit = QTimeEdit()
time_edit.setTime(QTime.currentTime())
Here are some commonly used methods of the QTimeEdit class:

setTime(time: QTime) -> None	Sets the current time value displayed in the QTimeEdit.
time() -> QTime	Returns the selected time value as a QTime object.
setDisplayFormat(format: str) -> None	Sets the display format for the time value. The format string can contain placeholders like hh for hours, mm for minutes, ss for seconds, and AP for the AM/PM indicator.
setMinimumTime(time: QTime) -> None	Sets the minimum allowed time value that can be selected.
setMaximumTime(time: QTime) -> None	Sets the maximum allowed time value that can be selected.

setTimeRange(min_time: QTime, max_time: QTime) -> None	Sets the minimum and maximum allowed time values.
setDisplayText(text: str) -> None	Sets the text displayed in the QTimeEdit when no time value is selected.
text() -> str	Returns the current text entered in the QTimeEdit.
clear() -> None	Clears the selected time value and resets the QTimeEdit.
stepBy(steps: int) -> None	Increments or decrements the time value by the specified number of steps.
keyboardTracking() -> bool	Returns whether keyboard tracking is enabled. Keyboard tracking means that the value is updated as the user types.
setKeyboardTracking(enable: bool) -> None	Enables or disables keyboard tracking.
timeChanged.connect(slot: Callable[[QTime], None]) -> None	Connects a slot function to be called when the time value is changed.

/

Example:

```
from PyQt6.QtWidgets import QApplication, QMainWindow, QWidget, QVBoxLayout, QLabel, QPushButton, QTimeEdit
from PyQt6.QtCore import QTime

app = QApplication([])

window = QMainWindow()
central_widget = QWidget()
layout = QVBoxLayout()

# Create a QLabel to display the selected time
time_label = QLabel()

# Create a QTimeEdit widget
```

```
time_edit = QTimeEdit()
time_edit.setTime(QTime.currentTime())

# Create a QPushButton to update the time label
update_button = QPushButton("Update Time Label")
update_button.clicked.connect(lambda: time_label.setText(f"Selected Time:
{time_edit.time().toString()}"))

# add the widgets to the layout
layout.addWidget(time_edit)
layout.addWidget(update_button)
layout.addWidget(time_label)

central_widget.setLayout(layout)
window.setCentralWidget(central_widget)
window.show()

app.exec()
```

Output:

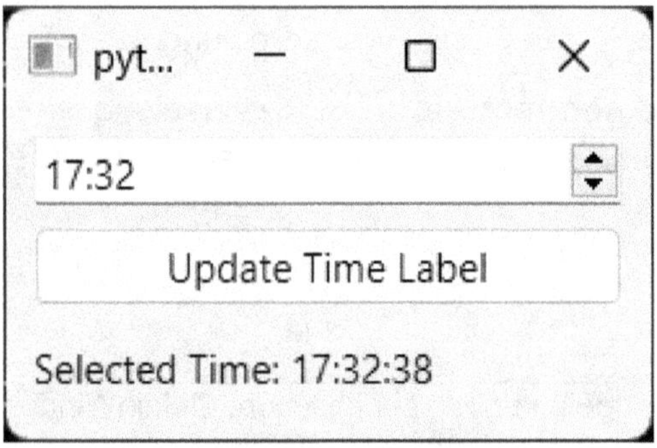

QTimer

In PyQt6, the **QTimer** class provides a way to schedule and trigger events at specific intervals. It is commonly used for tasks that require periodic updates or for implementing timers in GUI applications.

Here are some key points about **QTimer**:

- Timing Accuracy: **QTimer** provides a high-level interface to manage timers in PyQt6. The accuracy of the timers depends on the underlying operating system and the system load. Typically, timers have a resolution of around 10 milliseconds.
- Interval-based Timer: You can create an interval-based timer that triggers a specific slot or function repeatedly at a fixed interval.
- Single-shot Timer: **QTimer** can also be used as a single-shot timer, where the timer triggers only once after a specific duration.
- Signals and Slots: You can connect a timer's **timeout** signal to a slot or function using the **timeout** signal and the **timeout.connect()** method. This allows you to perform specific actions when the timer triggers.
- Starting and Stopping: You can start and stop a timer using the **start()** and **stop()** methods. The timer will run asynchronously in the event loop.
- Interval Adjustment: You can adjust the interval of a running timer using the **setInterval()** method.
- Timer ID: **QTimer** provides a unique identifier for each timer using the **timerId()** method.
- QTimerEvent: **QTimer** generates **QTimerEvent** objects, which are sent to the target object's event handler when the timer triggers.

Syntax:

Import the necessary modules

from PyQt6.QtCore import QTimer

Create a QTimer instance

timer = QTimer()

Set the interval in milliseconds (e.g., 1000 milliseconds = 1 second)

timer.setInterval(1000)

Here are some of the commonly used methods for **QTimer**:

start(msec: int)	Starts or restarts the timer wlth the specified interval in milliseconds.

stop()	Stops the timer. The timer will no longer trigger.
isActive() -> bool	Returns True if the timer is active (running), otherwise returns False.
setInterval(msec: int)	Sets the interval of the timer to the specified value in milliseconds.
interval() -> int	Returns the current interval of the timer in milliseconds.
setSingleShot(singleShot: bool)	Sets whether the timer is a single-shot timer. If set to True, the timer will trigger only once; if set to False (default), the timer will trigger repeatedly at the specified interval.
isSingleShot() -> bool	Returns True if the timer is a single-shot timer, otherwise returns False.
setTimerType(timerType: QtCore.Qt.TimerType)	Sets the timer type to one of the values from the QtCore.Qt.TimerType enum: PreciseTimer, CoarseTimer, or VeryCoarseTimer.
timerType() -> QtCore.Qt.TimerType	Returns the current timer type.
timerId() -> int	Returns the unique identifier for the timer.
remainingTime() -> int	Returns the remaining time until the next timeout in milliseconds. If the timer is inactive, it returns -1.

Example (This is the same example as for **QProgressBar**):

```
from PyQt6.QtWidgets import QApplication, QWidget, QProgressBar,
QVBoxLayout, QLabel
from PyQt6.QtCore import QTimer

# Create a QApplication instance
app = QApplication([])

# Create a QMainWindow
window = QWidget()

# create a layout
my_layout = QVBoxLayout()

label1=QLabel("This is a QProgressBar")
label2=QLabel("Counting up to 100%")

# Create a QProgressBar and set its range
progress_bar = QProgressBar()
progress_bar.setRange(0, 100)

# Add the widgets to the layout
my_layout.addWidget(label1)
my_layout.addWidget(progress_bar)
my_layout.addWidget(label2)

# Set the main layout of the window
window.setLayout(my_layout)

value = 0

def update_progress():
        value = progress_bar.value()
        value += 1
        progress_bar.setValue(value)

timer = QTimer()
timer.timeout.connect(update_progress)
timer.start(100)  # Update every 0.1 second

# Show the main window
window.show()
```

```
# Start the application event loop
app.exec()
```

Output:

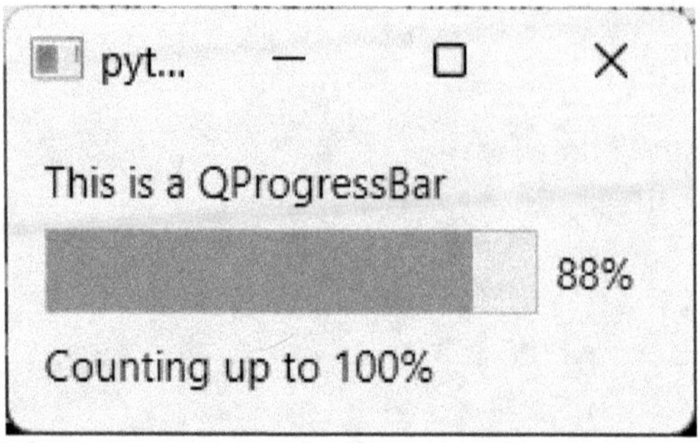

QToolBar

QToolBar is a widget that provides a customisable toolbar that can be populated with various types of widgets and actions. It is typically used to create a toolbar with buttons, icons, and other interactive elements for quick access to frequently used actions in an application.

Here are some key points about **QToolBar**:

- Toolbars can contain various widgets, such as buttons, comboboxes, line edits, and other custom widgets, to provide a range of functionality to the user.
- Actions (**QAction**) can be added to a toolbar to associate specific tasks or commands with toolbar buttons. Actions can have icons, text, tooltips, and keyboard shortcuts.
- Toolbars can have different display styles for their buttons, such as icons-only, text-only, or both icons and text. This can be controlled using the **QToolBar.setToolButtonStyle()** method.
- Toolbars can be docked to different areas of the main window, such as the top, left, right, or bottom. The docking behavior can be controlled using the **QToolBar.setAllowedAreas()** method.
- You can add a toolbar to a **QMainWindow** using the **QMainWindow.addToolBar()** method, specifying the toolbar's position or area.
- Toolbars can be movable by the user, allowing them to be repositioned within the allowed areas of the main window. The movability of the toolbar can be controlled using the **QToolBar.setMovable()** method.
- Toolbars can have separators to visually group related actions or provide spacing. Separators can be added using the **QToolBar.addSeparator()** method.
- Toolbars can be hidden or shown programmatically using the **QToolBar.hide()** and **QToolBar.show()** methods.

Syntax:

Import all the modules you need e.g.:

from PyQt6.QtWidgets import QApplication, QMainWindow, QToolBar
from PyQt6.QtCore import Qt
from PyQt6.QtGui import QIcon, QAction

create a toolbar and add widgets / actions to it:

my_toolbar = QToolBar()

my_toolbar.addAction(action1)

add the toolbar to the window

window.addToolBar(Qt.ToolBarArea.TopToolBarArea,my_toolbar)

Here are some commonly used methods of the **QToolBar** class:

addAction(action: QAction) -> QAction	Adds a QAction to the toolbar.
addWidget(widget: QWidget) -> None	Adds a widget to the toolbar.
addSeparator() -> None	Adds a separator to the toolbar.
insertAction(before: QAction, action: QAction) -> QAction	Inserts an action before another action in the toolbar.
insertWidget(before: QWidget, widget: QWidget) -> None	Inserts a widget before another widget in the toolbar.
insertSeparator(before: QAction) -> None	Inserts a separator before the specified action in the toolbar.
removeAction(action: QAction) -> None	Removes an action from the toolbar.
widgetForAction(action: QAction) -> QWidget	Returns the widget associated with the specified action.
toggleViewAction() -> QAction	Returns the QAction representing the toolbar's visibility toggle action.
setToolButtonStyle(style: Qt.ToolButtonStyle) -> None	Sets the tool button style for the toolbar.
setOrientation(orientation: Qt.Orientation) -> None	Sets the orientation of the toolbar (horizontal or vertical).
setMovable(movable: bool) -> None	Sets whether the toolbar is movable by the user.
setAllowedAreas(areas: Union[Qt.ToolBarArea, Qt.DockWidgetArea]) -> None	Sets the allowed docking areas for the toolbar.
setVisible(visible: bool) -> None	Sets the visibility of the toolbar.

Example:

```
from PyQt6.QtWidgets import QApplication, QMainWindow, QToolBar,
QPushButton
from PyQt6.QtCore import Qt
from PyQt6.QtGui import QIcon, QAction

app = QApplication([])
window = QMainWindow()

# create Icons from existing files
icon1 = QIcon("car.png")
icon2 = QIcon("train.png")
icon3 = QIcon("house.png")

# create and label buttons
button1 = QPushButton("Button 1")
button2 = QPushButton("Button 2")
button3 = QPushButton("Button 3")

# create and label actions
action1 = QAction("Action 1")
action2 = QAction("Action 2")
action3 = QAction("Action 3")

# add icons to Actions
action1.setIcon(icon1)
action2.setIcon(icon2)
action3.setIcon(icon3)

# create toolbar with buttons
toolbar1 = QToolBar()
toolbar1.addWidget(button1)
toolbar1.addWidget(button2)
toolbar1.addWidget(button3)

# create toolbar with actions
toolbar2 = QToolBar()
toolbar2.setToolButtonStyle(Qt.ToolButtonStyle.ToolButtonTextBesideIcon)
toolbar2.addAction(action1)
toolbar2.addAction(action2)
toolbar2.addAction(action3)
```

```
# add the toolbars to the window
window.addToolBar(Qt.ToolBarArea.TopToolBarArea,toolbar1)
window.addToolBar(Qt.ToolBarArea.LeftToolBarArea, toolbar2)

window.show()
app.exec()
```

Output:

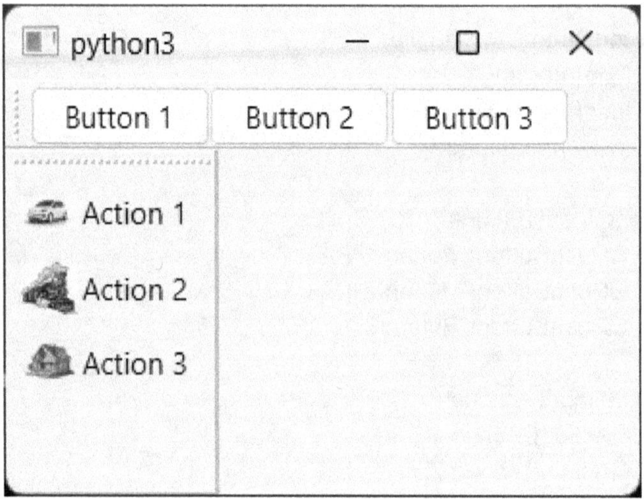

Jokes

There are many who would say that the whole subject of computer programming is a bit dry and there are others who say "if Paul had meant his book to be funny he would have put a joke in it".

So here we go:

Why did the Database Admin (DBA) get divorced?

Because the DBA had one to many relationships.

—

How did the software developer die in the shower?

He read the shampoo bottle instructions: Lather. Rinse. Repeat

—

How does a software code become unreadable?

No comment.

—

A SQL query goes into a bar, walks up to two tables and asks, "Can I join you?"

—

Why did the programmer quit his job?

Because he didn't get arrays

—

I've created a writing software to rival Microsoft.

It's their Word against mine.

—

I went to a street where the houses were numbered 8k, 16k, 32k, 64k, 128k, 256k and 512k.

It was a trip down Memory Lane.

—

Programming is like sex. One mistake and you have to support it for the rest of your life.

—

Two bytes meet. The first byte asks, "Are you ill?"

The second byte replies, "No, just feeling a bit off."

Those jokes appealed to me but if you want a wider selection, try this :

pip install pyjokes

then a tiny bit of code like this:

```
import pyjokes
my_joke = pyjokes.get_joke() # get a random joke
print(my_joke)
```

Will provide access to a library of hundreds more jokes…

Pyjokes has different categories including neutral, chuck (Chuck Norris) and all.. You can specify the category of jokes you want to get by passing the category parameter to the get_joke() method. Here's an example:

```
# Get a random Chuck Norris joke
joke = pyjokes.get_joke(category='chuck')
```

And if you have time, why not create a PyQt GUI that produces jokes at the press of a button?

Afterword

I am writing this note to wish you success as you embark on your journey to learn **PyQt**. It is a powerful and versatile GUI library that can help you create amazing applications that are both beautiful and functional.

As you learn and practice, I encourage you to remain persistent and patient. **PyQt** has a steep learning curve, but with dedication and hard work, you will soon master it and be able to build applications that can solve real-world problems.

Remember that learning **PyQt** is not just about gaining technical skills. It is also about developing your creativity, problem-solving abilities, and collaboration skills. I hope that as you learn, you will also develop these important qualities that can help you succeed in your future endeavours.

In the end, my wish for you is that you will benefit greatly from learning **PyQt** and that it will help you achieve your goals and dreams. I believe that with the right mindset and attitude, you can do great things with this library and make a positive impact on the world.

Best of luck on your journey, and don't forget to have fun along the way!

Sincerely,

Paul Hill

London, March 2023

The End

Please watch out for my next book

or give my Tkinter book a try!

www.ingramcontent.com/pod-product-compliance
Lightning Source LLC
LaVergne TN
LVHW051230050326
832903LV00028B/2327